About the Author

This is the second book by the author, Gerald Gossage. His "Long Road To The Manse" has been successful in that it has caused much laughter, and praise as a really entertaining book, for he tells of his many jobs of work and experiences growing up in the nineteen thirties to fifties.

To reach college and university from such a poor start was miraculous. Would miracles continue through the future years? The testimony of this book is a mighty "Yes".

Early in this book he discusses just what a miracle is. And as he tells of the wonders of his experiences he is sensitive to the people, places, and the need for confidentiality, so you won't find dates, and names of those whose stories he tells.

Born in South-East London in 1924 to a poor middle-class Christian family, he became the youngest, littlest choir-boy, and grew up with a Church of England background.

Suffering greatly from ill health which kept him away from much schooling and from all sports, he enjoyed singing and amateur dramatics and won prizes for his knowledge of Scripture. He has always been a happy person, full of fun and has never lost his smiling happy disposition. He did not stay within the Church of England, but became first a Baptist, and then Congregational. Now retired he still works preaching and teaching, and doing what he can to serve his God and the people.

This book just tells of some of the miraculous events and miracles he has experienced among the people to whom he ministered, and his wonder that The Lord would choose him to have some small part in a life of a "Long Road Of Miracles".

The fruit that comes out of your life is not what you strive to do, But what you allow God to do with you.

(John ch 15 v1-5)

Gerald Gossage

LONG ROAD OF MIRACLES

By Gerald Gossage

Author of "Long Road To The Manse"
describing the adventures leading up to this book.

Published 2007 by arima publishing

www.arimapublishing.com

ISBN: 978 1 84549 170 3

Printed and bound in the United Kingdom

Typeset in Times New Roman 14/16

Swirl is an imprint of arima publishing.

arima publishing
ASK House, Northgate Avenue
Bury St Edmunds, Suffolk IP32 6BB
t: (+44) 01284 700321

www.arimapublishing.com

Chapter 1

I stood by the Motorway viewing the speeding traffic, how different this scene was to the streets of London I knew as a boy where the speed was often that of the horse and cart, and when the solid tyred General Omnibus, and occasional car was something to stare at. There has been more change during the last hundred years than any other period in all our history.

People often say that the change has been a miracle, my grandparents never thought they would see men fly, but they never thought they would see the horror of the First World War either, as life never seems to stay the same perhaps progress is a miracle!

Noticing now this endless stream of vehicles speeding along, I wondered, "where do they all come from and where are they all going?"

I started to imagine the stories behind each face that flashed into a one second view, before it was lost to me forever.

Here's a travelling salesman with the contentment of a fat order book, followed perhaps by another whose worried look betrays his unhappy day when everything has gone wrong. A happy couple next, with the reception speeches and wedding excitement still in their ears. A column of slower moving vehicles heading for the crematorium, each occupant closeted with their own sad thoughts.

Someone speeding to catch a flight, passing someone rushing home. A group going to a party, another dashing to reach a deathbed before it is too late. One going to a sports event, another to visit aged parents. They are all there! And we all take our place in the mad rush of life, each wrapped in our own important little world. We wouldn't notice a miracle if it jumped up and hit us!

On Friday, the last day of June 1961, there was a little black Morris eight travelling down the A5, towards London, with a smiling-faced little man behind the wheel, his lovely wife beside him, and the baby boy and seven year old girl, his family, in the back

Way behind them lay the City of Nottingham and an adventure which in one way had been the toughest four years they had ever spent, yet in another way, four years of absolute miracles.

They had journeyed to Nottingham four years before, by train, with the then three year old daughter, and only a few personal belongings, they had had nowhere to live except a very temporary room which another student couple were prepared to share, and they possessed no means of financial support, but were committed to stay there for four years. That did take a miracle!

They now had an additional son, and a record of God fulfilling His promise to supply ALL their needs, including the house they had just left, College and University fees, books, food, clothing and everything else including the car they now travelled in.

Somewhere in front of that little car was a removal van heading to the new Manse, the house supplied by his first full time church, on the borders of London and Kent. What he did not know was that ahead lay a life of severe testing, hardship and heartache, but also a life of joy, and many more miracles. This book shares some of them with you.

Others might not see this first story as a miracle, but for me it was one!

Chapter 2

THE GREAT DAY

My eyes flickered open to view the strange surroundings of the new bedroom; then they sprung open wide, This Was The Day! I had waited for it and worked for it for years, I had been crossing off the days on the calendar for months waiting for this day.

It would be the greatest day of my life! bringing the realisation of many years of past hopes and dreams.

It was the fulfilment of a conviction that this was my destiny, and the springboard of hope in my future.

It was comparable with a young maiden's Wedding Day, or the Royal Coronation; The day that climaxed a long eventful and hard life leading up to it. It was simply called "My Ordination Day."

I would be recognised and set aside as a man of God's calling.

Great and important people travelled long distances to have their part in this special occasion. The Congregational Church at Belvedere was packed from floor to ceiling with warm hearted fellow Christians, and the flow of love from them all, gave it an atmosphere which could only be experienced, never described or explained. It was electric! Wonderful.

Of that 8th day of July in 1961 I will say little. A very good friend, Basil Carter, recorded the whole impressive act of worship on a tape recorder for me, and from time to time down the years I have listened to that tape recording, and it has been a help and encouragement through tough and discouraging times, and a happy reminder of the greatest day of my life.

I had started out as a person who had absolutely nothing: Poorly educated, untrained, useless and aimless; then a power beyond my comprehension took me in hand, fashioned me, educated and trained me, and called me to the greatest task anyone can undertake, a lifetime of service to the Eternal God and to His people.

I was reminded that once Jesus had taken a rough and ordinary fisherman called Simon Peter, and brought him to the distinction of being The Apostle, Peter. Not that I could ever be like him!

In my last book *"Long Road To The Manse"* I have told the story of the events leading up to this day. Now the day had come! I knew that God Almighty had called me to be a Minister of His Gospel, I felt humility and awe. This was the day when the whole church, with all its denominations, would recognise that call, and would set me aside for service. Representatives from the main Christian denominations were present and brought greetings, and took part.

The lusty singing of great hymns in a packed church is an experience that uplifts all present. The heartfelt prayers were golden communications with The Almighty, The reading of God's Word went home to the heart, and the messages to both people and Minister were so uplifting.

But the centre of that wonderful impressive service was when, having made my solemn vows, I knelt for the Ordination Prayer, with representatives of the whole Christian church encircling me, laying their hands upon my head, commissioning to the call that God had for me, and seeking the Holy Spirit for the life that was to be under the authority of God alone, in this special call.

It was a day that I, and others, will remember and cherish.

Sometimes there is preparation for a miracle, I was prepared for that special day

Before this great day I had been in much prayerful thinking about this my future life. Out of this meditation came some very real and personal decisions. One was that I accepted to wear The Clerical Collar as the badge of my new office. While the Collar has the advantage that other people know who you are, for me it was something that was to remind me of the great honour and high responsibility of being a servant of God.

I was determined to be a good advert for the collar I wore. Like a Salvation Army Uniform it says 'this is a Christian' and, sadly, people often wrongly judge God by those who are called His disciples. It has been a kind of pact I have with my Lord that as I represent Him, He will enable me to be a good advert. I think it has worked well down the years.

There is the funny story told, that two deacons went to a railway station to meet the visiting preacher who was to conduct their Sunday services. As the passengers alighted from the train it was soon obvious that none were wearing a clerical collar. "Which one do you think is a minister?" asked one deacon.

"I think it is this man coming toward us now" replied the other.

"Excuse me! Are you the Reverend Jack Smithers?"

"No," came the reply, "it's just that I am in pain with dreadful indigestion".

The idea that Christians look serious or miserable seemed so wrong to me, we have a great God, our rejoicing should show in our face, after all, living with God is just wonderful, we should try to let this side of living overrule the sad side, when we often share human sorrows and grief.

I made up my mind I would always remember that God was with me; I would talk to Him in my mind, and have a happy expression on my face.

Over the years it has become a successful habit and has paid off.

So much so, that when I later served as a hospital chaplain, one of the hospital patients asked a nurse if she could please see the chaplain. "Which one? We have a Roman Catholic chaplain, a Church of England chaplain and a Free Church chaplain." she was told "Oh, I don't know about all that, it's that little smiley man I want to see" she replied. And they knew who to send for!

Somehow the story got about and I was often called the little smiley man after that, and I took it as one of the greatest compliments The Lord could have thrown my way.

There have been many changes within the church since that ordination day when I became a full-time Minister, we have changed the way we sing, worship, pray, and the version of scripture we read.

I am thankful that we have almost got away from the antiquated First Elizabethan language, with its Thees, Thous, and Doths; although old habits die hard for some older people. But for me, as I have grown nearer and nearer to my Father in heaven, I have known how much He hates any insincerity on my part, so we talk together in the normal language that is me.

If I should slip into the old way learned as a child saying something like "Thy will be done O Lord" My Heavenly Father will immediately pull me up and say "Formal today aren't we?" which quickly makes me say with a smile "Sorry Father" and get back to being just me. Sincerity is vital in any relationship, especially the relationship between us and our God.

So, *'LONG ROAD OF MIRACLES'* The title of this second book will tell just some of the really great things God has done through this ministry that started that Ordination Day. It will also contain some of the things that happened which you might not think of as miracles. Do miracles have to be spectacular?

But there is one thing I must do before I share my stories. I must define my term 'Miracle'. I suppose that a miracle is some wonderful happening where we cannot understand how it could take place. It is not that it is impossible, for we acknowledge its happening, but the HOW or maybe the WHY of that happening is just beyond our understanding.

When I was 'The Great Wizzoso' doing conjuring tricks on the stage, people did not know how my tricks were done (or I hope that they did not!) People might think, "How does he do that?" But these were not miracles, because those witnessing what I did had a clear understanding that it was my task to fool them for entertainment purposes, but that there was a logical explanation, which I knew.

If it were possible for someone to return to our world today who knew nothing of the world since they died in say- the nineteenth century, they would consider that most of our modern world was a miracle. Computers, T/V, Telephones, people flying, even electricity itself would be a miracle because they just could not understand how such things could be.

The miracles that I shall talk about are not impossibilities, because others and I witnessed them happen. I think of them as miracles because I don't understand how my Lord God did what He did.

In this sense there are many miracles perhaps in everyday life. Love is a miracle, prayer is a miracle, but we have got used to these working;

they are real to us, even though we do not know just how they work.

I shall now relate some true happenings as best I remember them, and it is all The Lord God's doing; if I feature in them it is only that God wanted me to be the channel of His Blessing, I am nothing, only the man of God, the servant doing My Master's bidding. This must be clearly understood.

Just one other thing, All God's Miracles are for good, never for ill. There are millions of stories from Old Testament times through to our present day, of God doing special things or miracles, but always in love. He is The Loving Father giving Good Gifts to His children.

The bad and evil things that happen are from the enemy, God describes as Satan or the Devil. We sometimes forget that there is a war on between the two forces in the world.

Healing, righting wrongs, supplying needs, bringing happiness, these are things from God. He never makes sickness, causes trouble, or hurts in any way.! So His people can all look to God in confidence and faith.

I am firmly convinced that there would be far more miracles experienced by us ordinary people if we allowed Him to do more by our greater expectation and faith; for He can and will hear and work through us and in us. It is we who limit God, not God who limits us.

The first story I must tell is about my own lesson of acquiring faith, without which God could see that I could achieve nothing of His will for me, as a new Minister.

In those early days of my ministry I frankly took the view that I had quite enough to do caring for a church that needed building up, and people in need, than to bother about what I saw as a few odd Christians who talked of spiritual healing, or faith healing or whatever it was called.

So, when my ordination was over, I set about the task of building up the church. I had great ideas, I produced a big new magazine with what I hoped would have an appeal to the general population, and this was delivered to hundreds of homes regularly every month by a gallant crew of church members.

Special guest speakers, new organisations in the church. New back up for the Boys and Girls Brigades, and Sunday School. Visiting, serving on committees, you name it, I probably did it. I was a very busy little man, and thought that that was what I ought to do.

It all sounds very serious, but it did have its happy and even laughable side, and this little aside will show you just what fun was there, even in my rushing around, trying everything.

Chapter 3

CHRISTMAS DUMMIES

When Christmas loomed ahead I searched for an idea to increase people's awareness that Christmas was a celebration of the birth of Christ. A Christian festival: My idea was to build a life-size tableaux in the church porch, where all would see it from the road. It would show Mary, Joseph and the manger.

With this in mind, I contacted a large local department store in nearby BexleyHeath and they agreed to my request to loan me two of their shop window dummies. I had great fun on the day I went to pick them up.

Of course I wanted one of the dummies to be male, to dress as Joseph. But they could only let me have two female dummies, so they said I would just have to disguise one with a beard.

I proceeded to take the two female dummies apart and to fit them, as best I could, into my little Morris 8 car. The only way I could do this was to leave some legs sticking out of the back window and have one head-to-waist bust sitting on the passenger seat beside me. With this load I emerged from the staff entrance of the store and waited for a gap in the traffic, and there waiting for me to pass was the press reporter from the local newspaper. He knew me, and he grinned at my load and made one or two "I see" "Ah-ha" remarks to me through the open car window.

When the local newspaper came out that week it had an article headed "Minister's Leg pull". The article went something like this: - "Spectators were surprised to see a clergyman driving through BexleyHeath on Monday with what appeared to be two topless females in his car, one actually sitting beside him; there were also bare ladies legs poking from the car rear window. The sight caused some attention. Men exchanged a knowing wink, old ladies nudged each other, but the driver sped on with a chuckle. They need not have worried for the driver's wife knew her husband had two female nude models in his car.

"The Rev: Gerald Gossage of etc, hopes to use the dummies as Mary and Joseph in a Christmas display, and assures us that the next time they appear in public they will be suitably dressed." There were many laughs and leg pulls! You just imagine what remarks I got. Life can be fun!!

The idea worked well enough, Shirley, our organist kindly spent much time recorded carols on a tape recorder, which caused people to look toward the church entrance; many came to the doorway to view the life size Nativity Scene more closely, taking up the offer on a notice suggesting that they enter the church for a prayer to God for their coming Christmas celebrations. In the 1960s most people acknowledged God in their life and were not ashamed to admit it.

There was a faith there to build on!

My Mother came to spend Christmas with us and it thrilled her to be driven to the church one evening to see the porch display, suitably illumined with spot lights. Then she then entered the church and saw the massive tree fully decorated, with parcels for the poor piled underneath, and heard the carols. I was moved myself to see the two women I loved. Wife and Mother with tears in their eyes looking at the Christmas beauty of the display.

How NOT to do it.

Knowing the reality of God's call to me I was full of such enthusiasm, that I worked seven days a week and all the hours God gave me. I pushed and strained and raced around from morning to night: And all this was following the four previous years of a real hectic and straining study life in College and University, and the running of a student-pastorate, also being a father and husband. I should have seen what this would build up to for my health, but my attitude was "I'm young, and God is with me, I'll be alright."

It never occurred to me that I was not supposed to rush around thinking up what I could do for God and just expect that He would rubber stamp all my efforts to serve.

I started getting indigestion, then pain. We went on holiday to a friend's caravan by the sea, and I tried to relax, but there was the wife and children to give myself to, after all I had rather neglected them lately. The pain got worse. I had to stay in the caravan while Audrey took the children to the beach.

On my own I prayed, I wept, I tried to sleep, but I knew that I could not last out for the whole week's holiday. We came home early and I went to see the doctor.

After examination the doctor sat me in a chair and talked to me.

"I can do nothing to stop what is coming to you, I will get you a bed in the local hospital and they will decide what course to take after tests."

"You are going to have all kinds of trouble in the future if you do not follow my advice from now on, you must take a day off EVERY week; I believe that is one of the commandments anyway. You MUST find yourself a hobby that will force you to give time to it and take you away from your work. And you MUST cut down your work load and working hours."

"It is Your life of course, but if you don't take my advise it will be a short life, but an unhappy one."

God was about to teach me a sharp lesson, but was also going to introduce me into a life of deeper

It sounds so simple now, but it was not long
ore I was tempted to change my mind. Did I
lly hear God talking to me? Was it not rather
re likely that I thought it all up? Psychologically
ld it not be well explained that I was scared of
operation, especially with poor chances of
ning through it, so my mind had tried to
nvince me I had better pull out?

People who heard voices from God were
cial people like Samuel or even Joan of Arc;
y were way back in history not ordinary people
modern days. The doubts just poured into my
nd.

On the other side of my arguing mind, was the
nviction and joy that I knew I had heard God and
st take His advice. It was a great reason for not
ing through with the op` anyway. Also the
ught that I probably had the same fifty/fifty
ance of living if I refused the knife anyway.

We all go through this kind of battle with right
d wrong I suspect, there is one sure way out, I
nd it then and I have used it many times since. I
liberately sat and quietened my mind and turned
ce again to The Lord, and spoke to Him again.
1aster, I know that You love me and desire my

faith, and more miracles. It was to be a long and
rather painful experience.

Within a few days my skin turned yellow and I
had jaundice, I was so ill that I thought I should
die. I went into the local hospital for a few weeks,
then into the big hospital in Shooters Hill for
weeks.

There they told me that my blood condition
was not Haemophilia as I had been told by Great
Ormond Street Hospital when a small child, but
something called Von Willibrands disease. It meant
that the blood did not clot well. They wanted to
operate on me but it would be dangerous until they
brought the blood into a better clotting condition.

Then came that certain day I shall remember all
my life: The doctor sat on my hospital bed, a thing
they never did as a rule!

"Reverend" he said, "We operate on you next
Tuesday." (It was then Friday.)

"What about the bleeding under the
operation?" I queried.

"We've done the best we can for you, and we
shall have a plentiful supply of blood to put back
into you, so you've got a good chance."

Chance? "Chance!" I gasped "Just what is my chance then?"

"Oh, I would give you a good fifty/fifty chance, so you need not worry. We shall need you to sign the paper giving your permission later on."

I watched his retreating form as I muttered "fifty/fifty!" A toss of a coin, heads or tails, live or die, I did not like the odds. "But I am a Christian! God will look after me.

Or, perhaps welcome me into heaven!"

I lay in that hospital bed for hours thinking of my fifty/fifty chance coming on the next Tuesday, and praying for guidance. It was a glorious summer day and I was allowed to walk around in my dressing gown, so I walked in the grounds, praying and thinking. "Lord, please show me how to think about this."

The next day, Saturday, I had a surprise visitor. The Baptist Minister, Ernie Reeve, from Forest Hill, who had married us, had made the special long journey to see me, and I was so glad to see him. I shared my news, he promised to pray for me, and we talked and prayed together. As he was leaving, almost as an after thought pamphlets and a small book on t picked these up just as I came out' thought you might as well have them.

The book and leaflets were continuing His healing ministry toda had in the days when He walked the the testimony of those who had beer scripture telling of this continuing wor I prayed. I walked again in the ground:

Then God spoke! I did not hear a words coming into my mind that I kne from my own thinking of them. I cann what He said now, I was more taken feeling of what He was as He spoke to the words that He said. But I recall a c where He spoke and I asked questions answers just so full of wisdom and l wondered why I had not seen what He for myself.

When the conversation was over I happy, and I knew I could go back at any talk to Him again. I now knew beyond a what I must do. I would refuse the opera just wait on God and trust Him for healing.

highest welfare. You know the conflict I am enduring in my mind, I want to do what is right and what is Your will. Please give me now peace of mind in Your love for me, and in Your own way and time show me what to say and how to respond when ever I need to make a decision."

I then spent a little time praising and thanking Him for His love and guidance, and closed the matter; I resolved not to think about it until I had to, and then I believed I would be led to the right way.

When Audrey, my wife, came to visit she was full of things to tell me. The church member who had been bringing her to the hospital for visits had driven out of the hospital gates last time into the path of another car, they crashed, "But thanks to what looked like a miracle" she said "No one was hurt". Someone else had brought her for this visit. We needed a new Hoover, ours had given up the ghost at last, we arranged for her to get a reconditioned one on Hire Purchase, and I would sign any papers if she brought them in.

Finally I just had to share my thoughts about Tuesday's op. When I told her that I might refuse it, she seemed relieved, but wondered if it was the right thing to do. I found I had confidence in replying that it was God who healed anyway, and He would choose which way to do it.

On Monday morning I was presented with the form to sign, that I would agree to the operation. I found myself saying that I had decided that the risk was too great and that I would not have it done.

This really put the cat among the pigeons! Three people, each more senior than the last, came to tell me that I must sign. I didn't! I was plainly in the hospital's doghouse for the rest of the day.

Tuesday morning came and I was faced with the decision that I either sign to have the operation or I discharge myself because there was nothing more they could do for me. I felt like a pompous parson as I said, "I am a Christian and I believe that Christ will heal me, and that the odds are far better than fifty/fifty with Him."

"I am really grateful for all that you have done for me, for your courtesy, and kindness. But I feel it right not to have this operation, I will go home as soon as I can get dressed and arrange transport."

As it happened I think I went home on the Wednesday, the doctor advising me to have complete rest and to seek to be readmitted if I got worse. Back home I spent most of the next few weeks either in bed, in a deck chair in the manse garden, or dozing indoors.

Chapter 4
REST AND HEALING

Slowly the yellow skin started to fade in colour, and itching and tenderness started to ease, I began to feel my strength returning.

But I did have appalling depression, and I could not help bursting into sobbing tears, and going through the depths of unhappiness. I started to pray about a hobby that would take me from work, but as I had no interest in sport, and seemed to have no real other interests, I got nowhere in my search.

Finally I agreed to start preaching on Sunday mornings only. Then at both Services. I was offered another caravan holiday for a late autumn week and agreed, but before I left I was told by Audrey that one of our men in the church would like me to visit him.

When I reached his house at first there seemed no reason for his request for a visit. When I asked him what he wanted to see me about he just said "Come up stairs, I want to show you something."

He showed me a small room with a model railway running around three sides of it. He proceeded to enthuse over his model railway hobby. "Your wife tells me that you had a train set when you were young, we wondered if you would be interested to start Model Railways as a hobby."

I said the one thing that you must never say to Model Railway enthusiasts. "It's a bit childish isn't it?"

He took it calmly. "Just look underneath" he bent down, and I did likewise. There were several hundred electrical wires used to work points, signals and operate the trains. "What child could solder up that lot?" he asked. "Look at this building, at this carriage, look at this" he warmed to his theme "Each built to a scale of 4mm to the foot, that takes patience." "See this scenery? I painted that to blend into the foreground." Children could not do this. Children play trains; men model a railway, run it to a timetable, and put it into a surrounding community.

An hour or so later I left him with a new look on my face. I was good with tools, I was experienced with electrical wiring, and I could do those things. I had found the perfect hobby for me, just what the doctor ordered, I thought.

I was to start the hobby by making every mistake known to the model railway world, plus some!

When we went on holiday I found a model shop with a sale in progress, so I purchased, of all things, an Australian Diesel Train Set; because it was going cheap! With little money and no knowledge I learned the hard way. Today I still enjoy the hobby, I have had articles accepted for publication in the Modelling press, I have appeared on BBC 2 TV at peak viewing time with my layout, and my hobby has been used to bring at least one young stranger into God's Kingdom. I did not see it at the time but God was teaching me about His love for me and just how I was to work for Him in the coming days.

After the illness, quite suddenly it seemed, my strength returned, I came off the fat-free diet, started putting on weight, I got back to work, advertising the fact that Monday was my day off, I should only be called upon if urgent. Of course it didn't work all the time but the principle was there, and the family saw me more often.

I continued to thank God for His healing, but the hospital's warning that my liver could be permanently damaged came into my mind more often than I wanted it to. The Lord knew about all this; so there was to be a further chapter to this story.

I began to get a strong conviction that I should leave this church, which would be a most unusual thing to do.

I prayed for guidance, I tried to dismiss it from my mind. After all I had only been there two years, it must be wrong to have such a short ministry.

In those days of Congregationalism we had Moderators, Ministers in an advisory capacity to help churches and ministers in each set area. I now had a letter from my area Moderator.

It was really about another lesson God had just taught me. That of how to handle money, but it played a part in the main story. So let me tell you about it.

As a new Minister I had to buy some new furniture etc when moving into the church manse, and this had caused me to obtain from the denomination an interest free loan. I had shared this financial problem with a trusted fellow Christian who had told me that the sure way to financial stability was for me to Tithe. (The Biblical teaching of giving one tenth of one's income back to God.)

With great reluctance Audrey and I started to Tithe, though I could ill afford it at the time. From then on the first tenth of my income was set aside for The Lord's use. From a few weeks after this, money had seemed to flow in and I had paid off all my commitments, and repaid early the Congregational loan. We have tithed ever since, and to put it biblically "My God shall supply all your needs" we have never known money worries since, although bringing up the family of four children on what was the very poor pay of a non-conformist minister was never easy.

The Moderator's letter was in thanks for this repayment, and encouragement for the future. He went on to say that I had experienced a really tough time, and that he had wondered if a quieter ministry might have to be considered in the future, depending on my health.

The strong feeling that I should consider moving to another church would not be silenced. I just had to take it to The Lord in prayer, for I did not want to go.

Having explained the whole situation to God, (as if He did not fully know anyway,) I waited for guidance. I expected Him to tell me to stay put and get down to my work!

Once again His voice came clearly into my mind. "You have only been here two years so you think that if you go now you will have been some sort of failure." Yes that was what I felt. "The last Minister was here for nearly thirty years, although he is now called home, the people still love him. All you were called to do was to prepare them for the future, you have certainly shaken them up and prepared them for change, yet given them a unity of purpose, you must now move on. Just Trust Me!"

I told the Moderator I would consider moving if he thought it right. He strongly advised looking at a group of three country churches. When I visited them I thought that God could never ask me to undertake such a work. I told Audrey "No way." Her reply shook me "They cannot possibly be as bad as you have made out to be."

I prayed again, Audrey came with me to see them. It was there that The Lord called me to spend three and a half years as the group's Minister.

As soon as I moved there I visited the local doctor for ointment for my skin trouble, and told him of my past history in hospital. A few weeks later he asked me to return to his surgery. He now gave me a real thorough examination and pronounced me fit. Efficient doctor I thought!

Some months later I needed more ointment so I visited his surgery again. This time, I was told that he was taking surgery in another nearby village; I could visit him there. I had to make a call in that village anyway so I said I would call in there. "Take your papers with you" said the receptionist, "he won't mind, and he will not know what he has given you without them."

I placed the folder of papers on the front seat of my car and set off for the other village. A dog rushed out in front of me as I drove, I applied the brakes and missed the dog, but the papers were spilled all over the car floor.

I stopped, picked them up, and because they were all about me, I started to look through them. The doctor had written to the hospital about my condition, and there was a reply telling all about my illness, the refusal of the operation, and their concern that the liver might develop something, which could be serious. (With much medical terms that I did not understand) There was also a reply from the doctor to the hospital saying that he had given me a thorough examination and that there was no sign of damage to the liver, in fact I was very fit.

I only just made it to the surgery in the next village, for I spent some time in Thanksgiving and praise on the way there. A car is such a lovely place in which to pray.

In this situation my Lord had healed me directly; I hasten to add that I would not advocate avoiding doctors and hospitals thinking that God will always heal by faith. We are told in scripture to honour the doctor, and God certainly uses our medical profession to bring his healing to people. To my mind this miracle not only healed my body, but showed me how to live, and gave me a stronger faith. Essential equipment for the work I was to have to do later.

I now settled down to my new work in a country area. Being born in South East London and always living city life I found I was extremely ignorant of country ways. My first reaction was to pull these slow country people out of their country ways and put a bit of pep into their lives: But they were very patient with me, and I slowly learned that, to my amazement, their ways were better. I slowed down a bit, and it probably did me good.

Chapter 5
UNDER ORDERS

As I served in Christ's Church, I soon realised that as a minister I could do very little to help anyone unless God was part of the deed. So, I was forced to my knees, because being alone with my Lord was the only way to approach the tasks I had to undertake.

This method of working became for me a daily experience of miracles. Whatever help, healing, or comfort people received I knew it did not come from ME, it was the work of a living, loving Father in heaven who used me, a willing apostle. It was like walking with Jesus and He saying what we would do.

I recall several times, when starting my day with the reading of scripture; I would look for something The Lord might put in my mind to take with me through that day. There would sometimes be nothing that seemed special, so I would take just one verse and commit it to memory as the verse for that day.

I remember one day that started like that, and later that morning I was visiting one of our church members. Ringing her door bell I was taken aback somewhat when she opened the door with "Oh! Thank God you have come, you're the answer to my prayer." (It is not often I have been called that!) We were soon sitting, without the usual offer of a cup of tea, and she was sharing an urgent and rather complex problem. "I have prayed" she told me "but I cannot see how even God could answer my need."

It was then that the memorized verse came into my mind, I could also understand the context of that passage that had been so dim when I read it. I was amazed, It was the perfect answer to this lady's problem. Shortly after, her anxious face was full of happy smiles, "Let's have a prayer to thank God." she said "And then I expect you would like a cup of tea, or is it coffee?"

It is easy to see how I began to rely more and more on God to do things, rather than look to my own understanding. I was not rushing about so much, and He did things so much better than I could!

Confidentiality is a vital part of any Minister of Religion, and therefore I feel that I must protect those whose stories I tell. For this reason I am not putting my miracle stories in the setting of any particular church in which I have served, nor am I using the real names of those who are part of the story. If someone entrusts a confidence to a Minister of God they must know that confidence will be kept. But I feel that if anyone does read this and know it is their story I am telling, they will be pleased, for it is to God we give the glory, and it might be of help to strengthen the faith of others.

The Lonely Lady

Whenever a new pastorate is undertaken one of the first things that a new minister does is to obtain a list of the names, addresses and telephone numbers of both church members and adherents. Members are those who have made a public profession of their faith in Jesus Christ as their Lord and Saviour, and have been received into The Membership of

The Church, and they are fully part of the church family. Adherents are those who come or who support in some way but have not so professed their faith, or sought membership.

Church members are usually the first to be visited by an incoming new minister, although, depending on numbers, it may take some time before the visit takes place. However some church members are happy not to be visited for they are not in need of pastoral care and are seen weekly anyway. They understand the needs of others who would benefit from the minister's attention. It is because of this that the adherents often get visited as a priority. The Church Secretary often communicating needs out of his knowledge of the people.

Mrs Caxton was on the list of adherents and no one seemed to know much about her, so I considered that an early visit might be helpful.

Her address was very difficult to locate. There were no roads leading to her small farm-labourers cottage. There were several field gates to open and close behind me, and long single track lanes and fields to cross before I reached her little cottage, I had never seen anyone so isolated before in all my life.

She was a very pleasant woman, bright and intelligent. I spent the whole of an afternoon chatting to her, and discovered that she was a very lonely widow with one grow-up son, he worked abroad in what was then known as, a Behind the Iron Curtain country. A communist area, but what he did I never discovered, it was dangerous to write letters to the West from where he was, so she rarely heard from him. If she did hear the letters often came in batches of three or four and were out of date.

She had no transport of her own and could rarely get out far without the generosity of some far away farmer, when she would be taken shopping for the essentials of life. She possessed a strong faith in God and knew her Bible, which was probably why we found much enjoyment in the many things we discussed.

I well understood why she did not get to church on Sundays when I remembered the journey I had just made to visit her; and I could think of no one who would be very happy to make this difficult trip across all those fields to collect her each Sunday and return her afterward. I left her, making a note to call as often as I could.

It must have been about two months later that I heard that she had been taken into a hospital some goodly distance from where I lived. To visit her would involve quite a journey, taking half a day at least, but I fitted it in and went to see her.

She lay in the bed, grey and looking very ill indeed. She seemed also to be in some pain. She was delighted to see me, and I spent some time with her; she seemed a little brighter as I left her with prayer for God's Blessing and healing.

About ten days later I received a letter from her, thanking me for going to see her and acknowledging that I must be a very busy man, but that she would dearly love to have me come again. So I went!

Her condition seemed unchanged but her conversation was very much centred on the things of our faith in God. Finally, she almost blurted out "Do you believe in Christian healing, that is, as it says in the book of James, the sick are to call upon the leaders of the church who shall pray and anoint with oil and the prayer of faith shall save the sick?"

"Yes I do" I replied.

"Then" she said almost exhausted by the effort "I want to ask you for three things. One, can you arrange for me to be made a member of the church on my profession of faith in Jesus? Two, Would you bring Holy Communion to me here in the hospital? And three, would you be prepared to lay hands on me and anoint with oil for the healing of God?"

I happily agreed to arrange all this, and left her with a smile of contentment on her lips.

Taking this request and recommendation to the Church Meeting, I explained about her situation, and it was readily agreed that she be received as a Church Member, I then arranged with the hospital for a private room to be made available for the next and special visit.

I took with me one of my Deacons, and together we waited for her to be wheeled into the little room. He told me afterwards that a strange thing happened to him as we started the little service. "You started with a prayer," he told me, and said "there are four people in this room now" and I looked around, "there was you, me, and this poor lady in the wheelchair, and then I suddenly felt a glow of warmth as I realised that Christ was there also, even though we could not see Him." It was an experience that I shall always remember.

We had the sacrament of Holy Communion, then I welcomed her into the full membership of the church local and universal, This was the second thing she had requested, I read the very passage she had quoted from the Epistle of James, I laid my hands upon her head, and I felt a warm, happy feeling as I prayed for her healing,

I made the sign of the cross on her forehead with olive oil in the name of Jesus. And in the stillness that followed I felt that the little room was filled with love.

When the service was over, I asked the Deacon to go and get someone to take Mrs Caxton back to the ward. And then I found myself saying something to her that I had not thought of saying. I seemed to speak on impulse. I warned her that following such an act as we had made, Satan often tried to make a person renounce their faith in what had happened or in Christ. "Hold on to your faith no matter how tough the going gets," I said.

I rather shocked myself in saying this, but did remember that I had read something like this somewhere, so said nothing more. She took my hand and squeezed it, saying "Don't worry, my faith will be rock hard. He is my dear Lord and I love Him."

Three weeks later I had another letter from Mrs Caxton. She told how she had been in torment for two weeks. The pain had been almost beyond bearing and nothing that the doctors could give her seemed to relieve it for more than a very short while.

She wrote of one night when she had been in such pain, and then suddenly it had stopped. Then a rather pleasant voice had whispered that the pain would never come back again if only she would admit that the healing of God was a load of nonsense and that she renounced her faith.

She had whispered, "No, I won't, because Jesus is my dear Lord, and I love Him." The pain had returned and she had laid there tossing in agony; muttering something about "Jesus is Lord."

She reckoned that she must have fallen asleep, or perhaps they gave her an injection, she could not remember. The next thing she knew was that she awoke, it was morning, and she was feeling fresh and happy with no pain at all. She had waited a few days before writing to say that all pain had quite gone, she was feeling good.

I could not visit her that day but I went the next day to find her sitting up in bed with three or four women grouped around her: On her knees was her open Bible.

At my approach the ladies scattered, and I was able to enjoy a happy time with a joyful Mrs Caxton who looked so much better. I discovered that those ladies and others in the ward spent quite a bit of time discussing the Bible, and that some had wanted her to pray with them.

Mrs Caxton looked a different woman. Her eyes were bright, she had no pain, nor did she experience pain again while she was in the hospital. Over the next few weeks I visited her several times, she seemed to be getting better every visit and she kept up her fellowship with the other women in the ward with Bible studies and discussion. Everyone called her "the life and soul of the ward." I just praised God for her healing, and looked forward to her return home fit again.

Then one morning while I was still dressing for the day, the hospital phoned. "Sorry to call so early reverend, but Mrs Caxton died early this morning and as we have no relatives' address we wondered if you could come down and deal with her things and see Matron."

I cannot describe how I felt. Numb, dazed, lost! I went to the hospital straight away. I asked to see her, and made my way to her remains in the mortuary. I prayed over her and committed her into the hands of her Lord, and also prayed for myself, for understanding.

I had promised to see the matron so I now made my way to her office just in the corridor off the ward. As I approached I slowed down, for outside the Matron's office I could see Matron talking to two doctors and a ward sister.

One of the doctors saw me and beckoned me to come. "This is the Minister who attended Mrs Caxton," said the sister. They all turned to me as I came and joined them. One of the doctors said, "What have you been doing to Mrs Caxton?" "Nothing" I replied, bewildered.

"Didn't you have some special meeting in private with her?" "Tell us, what did you do?" asked the other one.

I explained what had been done at her request, including the laying on of hands and anointing.

"Marvellous" said one. "You know what was wrong with her don't you?" asked the other doctor. "No" I said, "She never told me and I never asked."

"She was riddled with fibrous cancer all over her body, and we have never had to sedate her once except when she first came in."

The other joined in "she should have been screaming in agony, instead she has been the life of the whole ward... smiling, talking... I don't know how she did it."

I knew, but I couldn't preach at them and tell them, although afterwards I wished that I had had the courage to. Instead the Matron took me in to her office.

I sat in my car for a long time, full of mixed emotions. I prayed for understanding, and soon it came. Her time to leave this world had come, but her simple faith had been honoured by the healing of her pain. She would have had nothing to return to had she lived, if she had gone back to that cottage she would have died alone. As it was she had been with friends, and shared her faith, and brightened the lives of others while she lived.

I believe Jesus healed her through her faith in Him, and I call that a miracle.

Chapter 6
JOINT FAITH

Mr West was the church secretary in one of the churches I ministered in, and he and his wife lived in the house opposite our Manse. Every Sunday they were in church of course, they were a couple with great faith and loving kindness for everyone, and were well loved by all. I noticed that Mrs West would often have pain in her joints, and she obviously had difficulty in sitting, standing and walking.

The trouble got worse as the weeks went by, and her husband told me that she had great difficulty dressing in the mornings. As time went by her muscular pain and stiffness got so bad that we could hear her shouting out with pain in the mornings even from our house, as Mr West tried to unlock her limbs and get her out of bed.

The doctor and hospital could do nothing to help her it seemed, and soon she became house bound, wheeling herself from room to room in a wheel chair. And having to sleep downstairs. But she would not give in, and often when I visited she would be trying to do something like peel potatoes with the potato on her lap, and her now swollen hands struggling with a pealing knife.

Except when in great pain, she was always cheerful, asking about others and of things to do with the life of the church. One day when I was taking my departure after visiting and praying with her, she called me back.

"Sit here again" she requested. She looked closely into my face, and then asked. "Do you accept the bible's teaching on Christ's healing?" I told her that I did. She talked about various passages, including the one mentioned in The Letter of James, and then asked "Would you be prepared to come and give me Holy Communion, and also anoint me with oil and pray for my healing?" "Of course" I said. A beautiful smile broke on her face; "Thank God; Oh please make it soon."

Soon after we had a simple meeting together in their dining room, Mr and Mrs West and myself, but I was often to recall the words of that Deacon about the presence of Our Lord: I thought of it then and knew My Lord Jesus was there with us.

To say that the Communion service was ordinary would be accurate, but there did seem to be something very special about it. Then I laid my hands upon her head, prayed and anointed her with oil according to the scriptures, and then it was all over.

According to her own account later, apart from it being an impressive act of worship she did not feel anything at the time, but week by week she improved. Her hands could do more, there was less and less stiffness and the pain grew less. She started to leave her wheelchair more and more to get about on two sticks. One day as I visited, she asked me to make a note in my diary of a Sunday about three weeks away. "What for?" I asked "That is the Sunday I shall be coming to church in the morning, to give thanks." she told me. "We must all give thanks, for there are many who have been praying for me, people are so kind!"

The improvement in her condition was remarkable, but her husband confided to me that he did not think that she would be quite ready to go down the flight of steps leading from their house and to cross the road to church by the Sunday she had chosen. "She will have to get back up those steps after too, I don't think she has thought of that." he confided.

Came the Sunday, and it had snowed during the night with a thin layer everywhere. I watched the snow start to melt a little but it would still be slippery by service time. I went over to urge her not to try it down those steps. I found her fully dressed for her outdoor adventure. "Give me your arm," she said, and slowly and a little painfully the three of us descended the steps from her house.

She was a heavy woman, and her husband and I were fairly exhausted by the time we got her to her seat in the chapel, she looked as exhausted as we were, but the triumphant look on her face was a reward for our efforts. It would have been impossible for our prayer of Thanksgiving to be more sincere than it was that morning, and it came from the heart of every soul present.

A little unspoken prayer of my own was answered when four other men of the congregation took her across that road, up all those steps and back in her home after worship was over. But she was never to miss another Sunday worship (apart from being away on holiday) as long as I was there. To the best of my knowledge pain eventually fully went, and she walked perhaps a little more slowly but without discomfort.

How can a prayer, the laying on of hands, and a little olive oil achieve so much? The answer of course is that it cannot. But "with God all things are possible", and obedience to His will, and faith in Him, who can know or understand? I think of it as yet another one of God's miracles.

Oneness in Marriage

I was working away in my study one morning when that ever-insistent interruption, the telephone, for the fifth time shattered the peace and demanded my attention. As an independent church minister I was, from time to time favoured with the confidences of my fellow clergy, whether they recognised my sincerity in wishing to help, or saw me as A man of God, or just preferred to talk to someone outside their own denomination, I do not know; but it was a high privilege to be called upon to share confidences with fellow Ministers.

This call came from a local Baptist Minister, and by the tone of his voice I knew he was in real distress. He told me that he had a bit of a problem and wondered if he could come and share it with me. Of course I suggested that he come straight away, and the measure of his anxiety was shown by his eagerness to come at once.

Within twenty minutes we were sitting in easy chairs in the study, and I led him in a prayer for the presence of The Lord to guide us in our fellowship together.

"It's my daughter," he breathed, "she has been happily married for six years, and now her husband has walked out and left her! It seems that there is another woman, and he has just packed a bag, walked out, and gone to live with her."

We spent some time talking over the situation, his fatherly love was very deep, and he did not know what to say to her or what to do. We prayed together, and then I found myself saying, "They were married in the sight of God, they sought God's Blessing on their marriage, they are one. We must pray in complete faith that they come back together and find the love that they still must have for each other deep down."

We prayed on this line, and then promised to pray, expecting great things from The Lord. I asked my good friend to keep me posted of developments.

From time to time in the coming weeks he phoned me to say that there was no change in the situation. But we undertook to believe and keep praying. Then one day he phoned to say that things were worse, the husband had asked for a divorce. We agreed to pray with more urgency and not to doubt that God would bring him back to her and that she would forgive him and take him back.

The days went by and I found the situation constantly in my mind and prayers. The waiting was really tough on both of us and his wife. Then at long last I had a phone call from my Baptist friend. I could tell by his voice that something good had happened, he came round to see me and tell me what had happened, and this is the completed story.

The daughter's husband went into a cafe and sat opposite a friendly face. It turned out to be a Pentecostal Pastor. Soon they were talking and the pastor, seeing that there was a problem, invited the husband back to his place for coffee. Soon the whole story came out, and the subject of God came in. Some two hours or so after, the husband gave his heart to The Lord, and left the Pastor saying he had some urgent business to see to.

My friend's daughter was amazed to find her husband on the doorstep asking to come in and talk. He told her how he had just received Jesus as his Saviour and had come to beg her forgiveness. Of course he broke with the other woman at once, the husband and wife's love was renewed, and they later restarted their marriage with a special rededication in the father's church.

"Ask, and it Shall be given you, Seek and you Shall find, Knock and the door Will be opened to you." "Ask in faith, believing."

Two Church Deacons Healed

I had two wonderful Deacons, (people the church elect to serve in running the church) they were husband and wife. They were now retired and happy together in their life and enjoyment in serving their church, and this they did extremely well.

I knew that Mark had to go into hospital for an operation in his mouth, and on the morning that I expected him back home I phoned Irene, his wife to see if he had returned all right, and how he was.

"I think that it has rather taken it out of him." she told me "He went straight to bed and is still asleep." I phoned again for the next two mornings, but he was far from well and his mouth was giving him much pain and bleeding.

On the next morning I got a call from Irene. "The doctor came again yesterday." Her voice seemed anxious "Mark wants to know if you could come round for a word of prayer?"

Their door was opened to me by Irene, whose face showed pain. "What ever is wrong, my dear?" I asked. "It's so silly really," she replied "I went to sit down just now and instead of sitting on the settee, I sat half on the arm part and sort of twisted myself as I rolled over and I have hurt my back. I'm in such pain, I don't know what to do with myself."

When Mark entered the room I suggested that they both sit together on the settee, and after a brief conversation I suggested that I prayed and lay hands on them both for they both needed Christ's healing power.

With one hand on each head I prayed for them in turn, and ended with a short period of silence.

Suddenly Mark got up with great haste and with a muttered "Excuse me" he rushed to the hall cloakroom, where he made sounds as if he were being sick; which made his wife get up and rush to see if he was alright.

I moved to the doorway and hall, but with Mark in the toilet and his wife half in the open door, I could do nothing. She eventually looked up, saw me and assured me he was alright, I went back into the lounge to await their return, listening to their comments of a repeated "I'm all right" from Mark, and "It's all blood" and "Use your handkerchief" from Irene.

At last they both returned. "He's alright," she reassured me, "But Mr Gossage, look at me, I am running about, and not an ache or pain, The Lord has answered our prayers, my back feels fine." She did a little dance to prove it.

I was with them for another hour, during which time I first heard the story of how Mark had brought up clots of blood and the stitches that were in his mouth. His mouth, which had been very swollen, was by then back to normal size and there was no more bleeding.

As I sat over a coffee and biscuit, which Mark was afraid to have, I watched the colour return to Mark's face and heard his conversation come fully back to normal. Our talk turned to something that he had been reading and he happily trotted up stairs to get the book to show me.

While he was out of the room Irene said "It's a miracle, you should have seen him before you came, look at him now, and all that stuff coming up, I don't know! God surely does wonderful things, and I am not forgetting my own healing this morning I was in agony, but just look at me now, no pain at all." Our prayers of thanks were so sincere that tears of joy were on all our cheeks before I left.

It must have been a testimony to the doctor too when Mark phoned him to say "My Minister has been round visiting me, and The Lord has healed me completely, thanks for all you did and your concern, but you need not call back, I feel great!"

The doctor did call, a little after I had left. His comment was, "Yes, that has healed up quiet nicely, I don't think I need call again."

Chapter 7
MIRACLES OF A CHANGED LIFE

To change our thoughts from God's Healing works for a little, let us think about other kinds of miracles. We can get back again to healing later.

I dislike the word 'conversion', because of the overtones it sometimes has. People associate religious conversions with mass rallies like those in Dr Billy Graham's ministry; but the word does sum up the experience of change that has been going on in countless lives through out all history, and certainly since the three thousand were converted on the first Whitsunday. The birth of the Christian Church. (Acts Ch2 v41.)

Every Minister of God knows that this change does not take place through any effort of man; it is God Himself who steps into a human life and changes as He wishes. When one sees the results, one is witnessing a miracle. "The old things are passed away, all things becomes new."

The Scriptures tells us that Satan blinds people to the truth so that they cannot see and understand, this so often makes it a struggle for them to take the step of faith that leads to the glorious new life in Christ. Most people know that they have made a bit of a mess of their life, that they are far from perfect and that they don't make much of a job running their own lives. But they find it difficult to trust the one who made them, the one who knows everything there is to know about them, and who loves them passionately just the same.

When a person reaches out to God and they just start talking to Jesus, they usually get around to telling Him how sorry they are for all their faults and failings. They have not loved God as they should, nor treated other people well. Things in their life they wish were not there, the shameful thoughts, the envy, or jealousy, etc. And they ask for His forgiveness, then something starts to happen. When they know that God has forgiven them, for He has said so, and that He will never remember those past things again, they turn to thanking Him for His forgiveness, and cleansing. For He has promised forgiveness to all who sincerely repent. The past failures are blotted out as if they had never been. It is a fresh start, like being born all over again.

If they then ask Him into their life. To take over completely, so that He will make everything better new and different, the old life goes, and they become a new kind of person.

I have seen this happen so often in the past, They rise from their prayer with a new radiance on their face, and they start a new life walking with God in humble obedience and joyous oneness as they let Him run their life. The miracle is seen in the new life that follows.

As I write this, I have just this week had a wonderful event in my life which has made me understand this even more clearly. I bought a piece of electrical equipment, and with it there was only a brief summery of how to use it, and I found that I could not understand how the thing worked, try as I did. I asked my son Peter if he could show me how to get the best out of this equipment, and he not only showed me how it worked but managed to get a ninety-four page Instruction Manuel onto my computer from the manufacturers Webb site.

This would have been the end of the story if I had not forgotten what he had taught me and if I could have found the manuel, but although I spent much time searching the computer files I could not find it.

Now my son is a senior engineer with the BBC, and what he does not know about electrics and computers seems miniscule; so I got back to him to help me, and he tried to instruct me in what to do; to click this and that, and so on. But I could not locate the file with the instructions I needed.

Now this is the interesting part. My son finally said, "you will have to give me permission to take over your computer so that I can work it from my end." I said "Well of course you can take it over." "No" he told me "You will get a form on your screen that asks you if you will let me take over your computer and will have to say 'Yes' or 'No'." Sure enough up came a notice telling me that he wanted to take over my computer, and that I must agree, or say 'No'.

Of course I clicked the 'Yes box', and to my amazement my son living miles away took over control of my computer, and I just sat doing nothing at all, and watched while he moved the arrow around my screen, clicked this and that, brought up boxes of writing I had never seen in my life before, and after a little while, there on the screen was the ninety-four page document that could explain just how my equipment worked.

He later explained that there had been no trace of the one I thought I had on my computer, I had probably blotted it out. So he had transferred a new copy straight from the company's web site onto my computer.

I could see at once the parable. Our lives get hopelessly messed up and we, not knowing how to deal with the results of our failures want someone who knows all about us in every detail to come and take over and fix things.

God our maker knows everything there is to know about us. He wishes to take over, straighten it all out, and give us what we need in order to achieve our highest potential. But we have to ask Him and agree to Him taking over.

As the old Christmas Carol says "Oh come to my heart Lord Jesus, there is room in my heart for Thee". But He won't push His way in, we have to invite Him, and millions in every generation have done just that and been made New People.

As I have watched this happen to so many people I have come to the conclusion that this is the greatest Miracle of all. It turns lost souls into inheritors of The Kingdom of Heaven. I look forward to spending eternity with them all in joy and blessings.

I have been privileged to witness this complete change in many people of all ages and all kinds, during my Ministry. The oldest I knew was a man in his seventies whom I came to know through his landlady. His landlady and her husband were members of my church, and at that time I was leading a Bible Study Group every week in their home.

Sam, as I will call this elderly man, suddenly came into the room where we were holding the study group, but started to leave with apologies when he saw us all. He had forgotten we were meeting there. I called out to him to stay, asking him if he could help us by giving his opinion on the matter we were discussing.

At first he paused by the open door. With great reluctance. Then as I asked him to close the door, he give his opinion to the question we asked him. I asked him to stay, and he then sat on a chair right by the door until the meeting closed soon after.

The next time we met there I went and found him and asked him to come in, and he moved from a chair near the door to one closer to our circle. This happened each week after that, then he made a one off visit to my church on Sunday, and after that, never stopped coming to his dying day.

Within a few weeks of chatting over the things about Jesus he gave his heart and life over to Christ and became a completely changed man. He was not a bad man before this but everyone who knew him remarked on the wonderful change in his nature. A sweet-tempered, loving person, who never missed the Bible Study, Church, or a time of prayer, whenever he could get close to his God. His often repeated regret was that he had wasted most of his life without Jesus in it; But my! how he made up for it in those few years left to him, before he went to receive his crown of life from His Lord.

I mentioned Dr Billy Graham's ministry, and I would give tribute to his work worldwide.

While there were vast numbers of people who came forward during his meetings to express their interest, there would be many who never gave their lives to Christ our Lord. And some of those who were visited and counselled later changed their mind so turning away from God and there were no change in their lives.

Although this is undoubtedly true, I have been amazed at the large number of men and women whose lives were changed. Although I did not go forward personally at the 1954 Haringey Meeting, what he said lead to my looking afresh at my own Christian life and later entering into the Christian Ministry.

I have met quite a few people who had their lives changed by Jesus during those meetings, some being directed by God into full time Christian Service.

Having spoken of 'conversion' it is also true that many Godly men and women have never experienced a dramatic conversion. Slowly, bit-by-bit they came to know Him, giving their lives to Him over a period of time. Their faith is deep, and they show in their daily living that Christ lives within them. The change is not always sudden, sometimes it has taken years, but the miracle of what God has done, and man could not, is still miraculous. The story from Dickens of Scrooge is just fiction, but it has reality in the experiences of many all down the ages.

It is not our task to judge others of course, Our Lord ordered us not to judge; but we do discover that not everyone in church membership or even called to a special position within the church is walking close to Jesus Christ, or Born Again, as Jesus called it. (John 3v3) Who knows just where another person is in relationship to God?

Chapter 8
A LIFE CHANGES

I recall a woman in membership of a church in which I ministered, who the church had called to be a Deacon. She would have been in her late twenties or early thirties and had a responsible position as a fully qualified vet' and Partner in a veterinary practice. She owned a lovely sports car and nice home and seemed to be nicely settled in life.

To the best of my knowledge God started to reach out to her through my preaching and the bible study group I was running. She called on me one day and we spent some time in discussion about the Christian Faith. She believed in Jesus and showed it in her life but she had never imagined that she could have a really close relationship with Him. Following this discussion she later called again and in my presence she prayed, and gave her heart and life to Jesus anew.

Several phone calls and visits later she became convinced that her Lord was calling her to the overseas mission field. She contacted a number of Missionary Societies only to find that none were interested in a fully trained and practising vet.

After a while she was so sure that Jesus was calling her to go into the overseas mission field that she gave up her work in the practice and entered a bible training college for missionary work, all this at her own expense of course and at great sacrifice. The course was long and hard, and involved her making many sacrifices, but she was convinced she was doing what The Lord wanted.

I had neither encouraged nor discouraged her, as I could find no direct guidance on the matter from my prayers. (I recall that Elisha had the same experience. II Kings.4v27) The day came when she passed her examinations and left the college. There followed months of waiting for God to lead, while she applied to several Missionary Societies for work involved with animal welfare or where a vet would be needed. There was a need for teachers, nurses, doctors and leaders, but nowhere was there a need for a vet it seemed.

Of course it was not easy for her to hold on to her faith when no answers seemed to come. Would God lead her just where He wanted her to go? However, the reward finally came. She was called to work in a faith mission (Africa Inland Mission)

Before she was accepted she had to raise enough cash support for her to be kept in the work. She had nothing left of her own, having sold everything to get this far: but support came from one church and another, from various Christian people, and the day came when she left for her life's work as a missionary.

First to France to learn the language, and then to a tough work just off the coast of Africa. She spent her life in this work, Teaching the locals the care of their animals, healing them, also having a work in the local church and teaching in the Sunday School.

After many years work, she retired, only a few years ago, and I am in touch with her still as she continues to serve her local church back here in Britain. Who can know what her life has achieved and what influences she had had on the lives of many others.

Who knows what God will do with any of us if we give ourselves completely to Him without reserve. We don't look for any reward save that of serving God and our fellow beings.

Little Miracles in Daily Life

Miracles do not have to be spectacular, they can be seen in our everyday life, If we Notice Them!

My wife was shopping in the near by village shop, and I was waiting to drive her home. I looked around, and saw Harry sitting in his wheel chair parked beside a public seat. The seat had obviously been placed in just the right place, for from it one could see nothing but beautiful countryside as far as the eye could see.

I walked over and sat on the seat gazing at the view. "What a fantastic view, Harry" I remarked to him.

He said nothing for a moment. Then he told me a story that I would remember all my life, and I would retell again and again.

"Three weeks ago there was someone else came and sat right where you are sitting now, do you know who that was?"

"I haven't a clue, Harry, Who was it?"

"The Duke of Grafton. And he said pretty much what you just said. Then he said, 'Harry, you see all that beautiful countryside? I own all that land, every bit of that land that you can see is mine!'

"And I said to him, 'I'll tell you something, sir. One day I shall own as much land as you.'

"'Don't be silly man,' he says, 'How could you ever own as much as that?'

"I said 'One day, sir, we shall both own just six feet of it.'"

That is something for us all to think about!

We only have this one life, what will we have achieved by the time we bow before our maker?

Looking back now at that country ministry I see a strange mixture of town and country in my life. From the peaceful dealings with men like Harry, to my own organisation of Sunday when I would visit the Sunday School children before conducting the 11am service in the church where we lived at Potterspury, Northants.

After lunch I would conduct afternoon worship at the church in Yardley Gobion, going on to Paulerspury to take a 5-15pm Service, and then journey back down the A5 road at 6-15, picking up elderly ladies and arriving back to take the 6-30pm Service at Potterspury. Returning the old ladies home after the service was over.

Was I ever late for the last service? Only once or twice, but the Church Secretary would start them off singing the first hymn, and there was a tape recorder in the pulpit with a recorded prayer should I be later than that, but I do not recall it ever being used. (Country people didn't like those new fangled things.)

It always seemed miraculous that Ron, who was the local blacksmith during the day and busy shoeing horses at Towcester racecourse on Saturdays, would arrive smartly dressed at the Paulerspury Church for the services on Sunday and play that organ perfectly.

His big rough hands, callused and hard, would produce lovely music on that organ, and rarely a note out of place. When you come to think of it,

Hands are a Miracle creation, the things that they can do! Thank God for two hands.

Ron had made a wonderful front gate to the place where he lived, and it was like an inspired sermon to hear him tell you about his gate. He had made it in his blacksmith's shop, and it represented "Weapons of the Bible".

He didn't just say, "There is David's sling and stone," He would say, "Now remember David? He took that stone there with four others. But he didn't need the other four stones, so they are not there. God only wanted one shot at the evil Goliath, but He did need David's skill and that sling. Wonderful what David and God did together. Delivered a whole nation. Just think what you can do working with God...." And so he would go through each of the weapons represented. Marvellous gate, lovely man. Surely such gentle godly people are a miracle themselves, but I'm glad he is no longer here to know I have said that, for he would laugh heartily at the idea of being called a miracle. But isn't everyone a miracle?

I visited the Paulerspury Church a little while ago, it is now run by The United Reformed Church, and they have completely rebuilt the interior of the hall, beautifully modernised, and they hold Worship in that hall while they tear down the interior of the church itself. That beautiful organ has been sold to a church in Germany I believe, and the whole of the church has been gutted to make way for a new modern church to serve the people of Paulerspury through the future years. I am not sure that this would qualify for the word "miracle" but it could never have happened when I was Minister there in the sixties, although I did put in a couple of modern toilets which blessed a few people .

Little miracles? Perhaps they are the ones The Lord loves best? I remember one morning awakening from a rather troubled sleep, I was just getting over a very nasty attack of 'flu, and the depression that I had encountered some time before came upon me making me feel worse still. My Morning Prayer time was short. "O God, just do something about this miserable sinner, please".

I had just managed to get dressed and down stairs when the front door bell rang. I shuffled to the door wondering if I had got to deal with a funeral. (Well, that was the mood I was in.) I opened the door to the radiant smiling face of one of the church ladies. She thrust something into my hands.

"I just had to dig these up from my garden and put them in this delightful little container" she grinned "The very first Spring Flowers this year, God only made flowers to say 'I love you' so let these say from Jesus 'I love you.'" With that she was gone.

I took them into the dining room and looked at them. What colour and detail there is in ordinary common Spring Flowers, and she was right, there was not much purpose in their existence other than to say "I love you." I changed my mind about not having any breakfast! I soon felt loads better. A miracle can start when someone says "Jesus loves you". The lady was saying it in a deed, I feel sure Jesus was saying it that morning, and I was cheered up.

Some people will find what I am about to say very hard to take. But if you think of the true relationship between a child of God and the all powerful and deeply loving Heavenly Father, it becomes easier to understand. Or just think of the simple or silly things a parent will do for a child.

I believe that God is just as keen on helping us with very little things as the great miracles. If I am repairing one of my model engines or fixing a piece of equipment, sometimes a small part, like a screw, will fall to the ground, and you know such things always seem to roll away to where you cannot find them. After looking in vain, I always ask The Lord for help.

"Lord would you show me just where that has fallen?" And I always, Always! Find it! And quickly!

All right, don't believe me, but it is true!

If I cannot find a document, piece of paper, or perhaps a book, I ask to be shown its whereabouts, sure enough I will find it soon after asking. Could it be that having found this to work so often I now just expect such results? Well you think whatever answer suits you, but "My God supplies All my needs..." He never fails. Perhaps you might like to try it the next time you just cannot thread that needle, or find that which you have dropped. Expect results and you will get them.

I remember a fellow student in college who went into C.W.M as an overseas Missionary. He told us that the African people with whom he served had such a great faith. The very first night he was there some natives came calling on him. "One of our elderly church members, a great Christian, is very ill, please come at once." they begged. He was soon shown into the old mans hut, he was lying on his bed surrounded by a crowd who were quietly singing a hymn.

"What am I expected to do?" enquired my friend to the church deacon who had brought him there. There was surprise on the man's face as he said "You lay your hands on him as the Bible says, and you pray him back to health."

As a new Missionary my friend was not sure just how to go about this, but he moved to the bed side, laid his hands on the old mans head and prayed out loud for comfort and easy of any pain or discomfort. Then He thanked The Lord for His presence with them and asked for complete healing. Others joined in with prayer, and many also laid their hands on the old man. My friend quietly left after about an hour.

The next morning my friend was amazed to have a visitor, it was the old man himself come to thank The Lord and the Missionary for God's wonderful healing. "You see," said my friend, "The Word of God said it, and they believed it would be, and it was so." They just took God at His word. A miracle?

To quote the hymn.

"If our love were but more simple, we would take Him at His word.

And our lives would be all sunshine, in the sweetness of our Lord."

Didn't Jesus talk about the faith to remove mountains?

Chapter 9

A PERSONAL MIRACLE

"Ask, and it shall be given to you."

I suspect that many of us still live as I once did, having a belief in God but living such a busy life that God almost gets shut out of our daily living. I am now fully convinced that this is not the way God intends us to live.

Jesus once said (John 15) that our relationship with Him should be like a branch living in a vine. The purpose of the vine is to produce grapes, and that cannot happen if the branch becomes cut off from the vine, which is its only source of life and power. When a branch is broken off no fruit can grow, and the branch just dies. "Live in Me" said Jesus "and I will live in you, without Me you can do nothing." Does this explain why we are so powerless at times? And why so many rarely think about God each day?

I am advocating a Christian life that is lived all the time in Christ. And it can be achieved, all be it with much application and practice at first. We have to bring Him into every aspect of our daily living, talking to Him constantly in our minds, and sharing everything, being always prepared to let Him steer our life, without our snatching control back when His way is not what we want. If we have this kind of trust in Him and live it out, living is rich in Blessing, and it can be most useful in times of need, as my next personal story shows. It also shows that Miracles are often centred in a solid Faith in God.

As a working Minister, my practice was often to come home for my midday meal. My wife at this time was out working, so I would get my own meal, eat it, take a brief break, and then to return to work doing whatever I had scheduled for the afternoon.

One day, with thoughts very much on someone that I had just visited, I came home for lunch. I stood in the kitchen asking myself what I would like today. I decided that I would boil an egg, so I switched on the cooker ring, got out the egg saucepan and filled it with water and was about to put the egg on to heat when the phone rang.

Happily it was a very short call and I returned to the kitchen to ask myself 'What was I doing?' It was at this moment that I remembered that Audrey had told me that she had prepared a meal for me and left it for me to warm up. Better than a boiled egg I thought!

I switched off the now brightly red glowing hot plate, emptied the water from the saucepan, and got out the prepared meal, popping it into the microwave. I moved to get something stored just above the cooker, and as I reached up to get it, with my full weight on my hand, I put my hand down upon the hot cooker ring. It had only just stopped growing red. I let out a scream of agony, and I rushed my hand to the cold tap, there was a smell of burnt flesh in the air, and I nearly fainted as the shock drove the blood from my head. I was also aware that I was shouting, or making a loud noise in my great agony. It truly was a bad burn.

I looked at my poor left hand. It was covered with circular red and brown wealds where the round elements had burnt into my hand and fingers. The pain was almost more than I could bear, even with the cold water.

What could I do? I wondered. With a hand like this I would not be able to drive to the hospital. Did I ought to phone for an ambulance? Then, I remember I shouted out loud. "You are a Christian, where is your faith, Call on The Lord for His help." I can still vaguely remember what I said and recall that my voice sounded strange as I still cried out words through my pain "Father! I am sorry that I have been so silly, I should have paid attention to what I was doing. Please, in Jesus' Name I ask for healing."

"Will you take away the pain, and heal my burnt hand." I recall pausing to think, it would be difficult to believe that He was healing me when I was in such pain. So I added,

"It would help a lot if you could distract my attention from this hand while You work your healing miracle."

I had barely got the words out when the front door bell rang. I hastened to see who was there. I stood at the door talking to a man who wanted something or other, and finally returned to the kitchen. "What was I doing?" I asked, and then I remembered. I at once looked at my left hand, "That's amazing" I said out loud. "Lord, You are fantastic." There was no sign of the burn at all. The red and brown wields were gone, and all the pain had gone too.

"Thank You" is such an inadequate phrase. But I remember that I said it over and over again.

A few minutes later I sat at the table eating the meal that my wife had prepared for me, with a knife and fork in my hands and feeling no discomfort at all: and I kept looking at my left hand, there was no sign that my hand had been burnt at all. I say that this was a miracle, I shall always remember it as such. And for which I shall always be thankful.

Other Kinds of Miracles

One of the Miracles of my first full time church was however concerned with buildings.

The previous Minister had owned his own house, and so when I was called to be their new Minister they had to find a house, called a 'Manse' for us to live in. The best that they could do in the time they had was a small semidetached house in BexleyHeath, some way from the church.

I was concerned about this as it was quite a distance for me to travel, and church people did not easily come to visit me. As a family we felt cut off from the church work and friends, never good at a new Ministry.

I prayed about this, but could not see what God could do. (A typical attitude in all of us.) The church had spent all that it could afford in buying this Manse they now had and as far as I could see there was no changing houses without extra expense. Also where could there be such a house closer to the church anyway? The church had tried to find one and failed.

On a second visit to one of the church members, who happened to have been recently widowed, he told me that he was moving away to be nearer his son. The house was too big for him now that his wife had died. During the course of conversation I asked about his selling the house. He had just put it into the hands of an estate agent.

"What a dreadful shame" I remarked, "This is just what your church is crying out for". "What?" he questioned. I said an inward prayer "This lovely large house, would be ideal for any family Minister all down the years to come. It's within a hundred yards of the church, an ideal Manse."

We talked further, and I winced a bit when I knew what the estate agent had suggested his house would fetch. "I could never GIVE this to the church" he said. "You don't have to, we would pay for it when we sell the existing manse." I warmed to my theme. "Just wait for a few weeks to see what we can come up with." That is just what he agreed to do.

When I took the matter to my Deacons they were very negative, but agreed to pray about it and look out for a possible buyer for our existing house.

I now found my prayers were positive, and expecting a miracle. As far as I could see it would be the last time such an offer would come our way, and the church would benefit in every way.

Nothing happened for a week, and then things moved rapidly. A Deacon said he knew of someone who was interested in buying the BexleyHeath house and a price had been mentioned. About the same as the church had paid for it in the first place. It seemed fair.

I again visited the owner member of the house we wanted. I gave him the figures I had worked out. The amount we should get for the other property, less legal fees and my moving expenses.

He looked thoughtful "I'll think about it". I quickly cried "Don't just think about it, Please, PRAY about it, it is important to your church."

He phoned me the next day. "If those figures of yours work out, I'll agree to sell to the church at that price. There won't be an Estate Agent's fee to pay either this way".

I was amazed at the speed that things moved after that. The negotiations went through without a hitch, and the solicitors moved faster than I thought they could. We were moving house in no time. That house still remains the Church Manse today, all these years after. The church has benefited from that sale in many ways, and it did not cost them a penny more to make the change over. God works in wonderful ways!

In fact, as a "thank you" present the dear man left behind a beautiful roll-top-desk as a gift to me. Later, when I was leaving the church to go to another, one of the Deacons insisted that the desk belonged to the church, so I moved it into the

Minister's vestry and left it there. It seemed the best way of turning the other cheek.

Of the rest of that Ministry, there were many ordinary miracles. I have happy memories of sitting with a young girl called Mona, who was confined to a wheel chair, and somehow we seemed to hit-it-off so well that I believe that she was really helped as she tried to bear her burdens as a disabled person.

I think there is a small miracle in bringing a little light and happiness to some whose lives are badly restricted, of seeing the happiness come to mentally or physically handicapped people by such a little effort by us.

I was also able to help poor and homeless people in the district through having a part in a society for the relief of local needy people, when I became chairman of that society. There was not only help at Christmas time, but those who hit hard times through the whole year.

A little personal miracle came when I had expensive troubles with that car I had brought with me from Nottingham, The local garage man offered to buy it from me in order to repair it and sell it. He put time and money on it and repaired it, when it was back in good order he stood it outside the garage for sale. In the end he sold it back to me for the same price he had paid me for it when I sold it to him. I could not understand why then, and I still wonder about it.

I had a generous loan of a car from a church member when I needed it during the time my Morris was off the road, so I did feel that God was looking after me.

I was to journey to the new Ministry in the country side in that car, and later give it away, because the new group of churches supplied a group car for my use.

I still remember from that first church the wonderful young people in the Boys Brigade and Girls Life Brigade. It was great to go to camp with them and share the fun as well as to have the opportunities to share my faith with them both on a personal basis as well as with a group.

Memories of happy weddings; of helping young couples in the early days of their marriage. There were lovely families that I was privileged to know and care for, often sharing important events and happenings in their lives.

Of course there were the sad times and the many occasions when sickness invaded their homes. To find some elderly soul in bed with 'flu or something, and be able to go and put their kettle on, do their shopping, or just talk and pray with them. Neighbours and friends were always ready to do these things, and the church members were often quietly going here and there on such loving tasks. But it shows that there are miracles of love and kindness always going on, and surely they are God guided.

Someone once said to me "I always thought that a funeral, was just a funeral, but after attending this one I know that a funeral can be a real help, blessing and outreach of God". I was pleased to hear this as few people would suspect how much thought and hard work goes into the preparation of this vital act of worship.

An hour or so visiting the bereaved family is not just finding out their choice of hymns, it has to be a time of drawing out their thoughts and memories of the loved one and gentle conversation gauged at helping them through what has happened, as well as learning about the deceased so that a proper tribute can be paid in front of family and friends during the service.

All this reminds me of the longest Funeral that I have ever taken.

The funeral was timed for 10-30am at the church. The fog that morning was so thick that most of the friends and congregation arrived late at the church; having found it difficult to see where they were going. By 11am the church was well filled. By 11-30 some started to leave.

Soon after 12-30pm the funeral party arrived at the church, and I took the service with a much-rumbling tummy. We started on the road for the crematorium at just before 1pm. The fog was still so thick that two of the undertakers walked in front of the hearse, one behind the other to give a gap of two yards before we might hit anything.

There were many stops to ease a way past abandoned vehicles, and more times than I could remember when we discovered that we were on the pavement because we lost the curb at entrances to houses. Once we had to stop because we had lost the following cars holding the family.

At ten past four in the afternoon we arrived at the crematorium, they were supposed to close at

4pm, but had stayed open late with the hope we would get there. The committal service over we left the crematorium chapel and as we left there at 4-35 the fog started to lift a little, and soon after 5-15pm I was back home with hardly any sign of fog at all. I had been at the church by 10am. So I had been away on that one funeral for seven and-a-quarter hours. The condemned parson ate a very hearty tea and dinner. What Both? Yes Both!

Chapter 10

GOD KNOWS ALL ABOUT CARS!

I mentioned in Chapter one that I was called to a Group of Three Churches; and. I drove from London to the Northamptonshire area in my little black Morris eight.

Cars? My Heavenly Father knew more about cars than the churches I went to serve in that country area. But mine had let me down several times in the past, and now that the friendly garage man had done wonderful jobs on it I had every confidence that it would continue to serve me.

The church Group had told me that they would supply a car but I did not think too much about it at the time of moving. Now I was told that I would find it in the garage. I was very curious to find out what kind of a car was there and soon found the garage key.

It turned out to be a Ford Popular. The cheapest in the Ford range. Perhaps I ought not to look this gift horsepower in the mouth but I soon found it to be noisy, and of rather poor quality. Worse still it had no heater, and winter months in the countryside became a bitter cold experience. It was not unknown for Church Members to make up a hot water bottle for me to take with me as I left them, and I would return it to them on the following Sunday when I saw them.

A journey with a very hot rubber bottle stuffed under your woolly is not the best way of keeping warm, your face, back and hands still keep frozen, and one hand is constantly needed to move the bottle to other parts of the body where the draughty car is busy lowering the temperature. If the journey was of any duration the bottle would soon be cold anyway, and there were actually church people who never thought to offer me a hot bottle at all. (Can you imagine any Christian not offering his Minister a hot water bottle when visiting?)

The result of all this was that I put up with it for a little while and then mentioned it in my prayertime to The Lord.

As soon as I did this, one of the deacons asked me, did I know that the car had not been serviced for some time and that I ought to find time to take it to the garage on the main A5 road, which was where they usually had the car serviced.

I had obtained my petrol and oil from that garage so I knew the garage man fairly well. I was about to know him better and later play quite a part in his life, but that was for the future.

The car was supposed to be in for the day, so in it went, but halfway through the morning I got a phone call from him, could I go and see him, so round I walked. Once the car was lifted heavenward, on the ramp I was invited to stand under it and gaze at its under-garments. It was certainly rusty! And the material that had once been respectable was now seen to have holes as if the moths had been at it. A poke with the screwdriver showered confetti like fragments, leaving slightly enlarged holes.

After ten minutes I was asked to face the fact that my suspension was lethal, my seals would have to be replaced, my body was in need of welding in a number of places, and to all this had to be added a major service which at this stage might have to include a few other expensive replacements. My front bearings were not a big job, but he would have to check the tracking, the tyres were worn unevenly, and would have to be replaced within six months or so.

I looked at him, "What do you advise me to do?"

"Well one thing I wouldn't do" he said "I would not drive this death trap while it's like this." That did not help me much!

He looked me straight in the eye, with a small smile on his face "I sense that you don't want to drive this car anymore, and it will be an expensive burden on the churches as long as they keep it. You were going to manage without it today, manage without it tomorrow as well. I'll loan you a car for Sunday, and if you are doing that funeral on Monday, the funeral director will supply you transport for that. He often does for the other clergy."

I became fascinated at the man's knowledge. "I know Sid West your Church Secretary, he'll be in for his petrol, and I'll show him what you have just seen and talk him into having another car. Something a bit bigger to hold your family and with a heater. I will put out the word that I'm looking for something, and with any luck I'll have another car for you within a week."

I had real doubts about all this. It was not my way of dealing with the matter. "I do have a joint deacons meeting Thursday" I mentioned "I'll report what you say, and I do appreciate your offer of a car for Sunday, I shall need that."

We moved to the door, for a moment I thought he was going to put his arm round my shoulder, but he dropped it just before it got there "I don't think you are the kind of person who would take offence if I speak my mind" he said "Now you are living in the country you are going to find it so different from town and city dwelling, I've lived here all my life, we all of us have grown up with each other and know each other. I know the chapel folk, they are the salt of the earth, and they will do what is right, but they don't take it too easy from any one they think of as a foreigner, a stranger, that is, we are a bit suspicious of city folk, too smart by 'alf! Tell 'em facts about this motor if you like, but take my advice sir, don't push, just let 'em come to things in their own way."

"I hope we are friends, sir." He faced me

"Friends for life I hope." I said as I reached down and took his grubby hand. The handshake was a warm one. And I was learning!

As I walked back through the village, saying "Good afternoon" to everyone I met, I just could not get used to the idea that I was a foreigner to them. Me! A foreigner! I was English not foreign. Were we not all the same? Looking back now over forty years I can see so clearly that I was a foreigner, I was a townie, worse I was a city dweller, far worse I was a Londoner, the worst kind of foreigner to the country man. No it is not an insult! It is a complete lack of knowledge or understanding about the way each of us live and think.

As a Londoner I never really knew or cared what Harvest or nature conservation was about, but I was amazed to find that there were people in other parts of England who had not a clue what a "tube" was, and would be hard pressed to name any so called famous London streets. We are all just ignorant of each other's way of life, and think that everybody lives and thinks just like us. I don't think that I learned that lesson while I was living there in that country ministry. I did push them into new things, and they would often smile at me as I unfolded my plans and ideas, but I don't think they ever went where they did not want to go, they did not change. But I changed… slowly!

The garage man had loaned me a car for Sunday and I returned it on Monday morning. "Can you spare me a little of your time just now" the garage man asked

"Yes, of course."

"Then come into the house" he invited.

I sat by his warm fire chatting to his wife and drinking tea. "I'm worried about Bert" she said of her husband "He works far too hard, seven days a week, just never stops. Work, work, is all he thinks about". She confided "Last year I got him to close the garage on Sundays, and would you believe it they were knocking of our door all day with faults, or a puncture, or even petrol".

Fifteen minutes passed like a flash, then Bert put his head round the door "Finished your tea, Mr Gossage?"

"Yes thank you."

"Then come and have a look at this." On the forecourt was a pale green Ford Consul, it looked lovely.

"Have a drive round in this and tell me if you'd like this as your ministerial car?" He showed me under the bonnet, and we looked all over it.

"How much is it?" I asked.

"We'll talk about that only if you like it, I don't want you to have something you are not happy with." I took it for a test drive!

"I just love it." I told him on my return "How much is it?"

"I just don't know at the moment." He replied. "When you called in I put through a phone call and asked a friend of mine to bring it down while you waited. If you like it I will find out whether you can have it, and put the word about among your church folk, just leave it to me for the present." I returned home with very mixed feelings!

On Tuesday morning Sid West, the Church Secretary, came over to see me. "That big Ford Consul you were driving about in yesterday like Lord Nuffield, do you like it?"

"Yes I do, but Burt wouldn't tell me how much they wanted for it."

"Quite right too" was Sid's comment "Nothing to do with you, that is for the Finance Committee to bother about, you just get on with your sermon preparations; we want another one as good as last Sunday's." The glint in his eye was wicked! "You are taking a Bible Study at Yardley tonight?"

"Yes."

"Well, two of your flock will be absent, they will be at my house for a special finance committee meeting, so don't go sick visiting them." I got the message, loud and clear, and I loved him for the way he delivered it.

Talk about jungle drums! Suddenly everyone seemed to know I was without transport, and I was offered lifts to meetings, and even the loan of someone's car for the day. The phone just kept ringing with offers.

On Saturday morning Sid came over the road to see me. "Can't have everything we want I suppose" he said with a rather sad face "But we have sorted out your transportation problem, Bert at the garage has done the best he could. You better come over to the garage and see what he has done". I started to walk toward the gates.

"Where are you going?" Sid called "Not Bert's garage, your Manse garage". He walked over and opened our garage door, there stood the Ford Consul. I could have hugged the man! He allowed himself a big grin!

And I was never offered a hot water bottle for winter driving again.

Bert and I became friends, and I was always mindful of what his wife had told me about her concern for his health. I discovered that Bert was very keen on fishing, and with the help of his wife I hatched a plot with two men who used to go fishing with him years before. The result was that we did some notices 'GARAGE CLOSED TODAY' which we put around the garage, and got Bert off on a local fishing trip with his old buddies for a whole day one Sunday.

Perhaps it was just the right thing to do, for Bert realised that the worry of running the garage, being at the beck and call of every motorist in trouble, on top of the finance and bookkeeping, form filling, and dozens of other things he was doing was not doing his health much good.

One winter he was forced to close up for two weeks when he had 'flu. And it really pulled him down. So his wife and I, and no doubt a few others, started on at him to give up the garage.

It was an impossible idea to him at first, but seemed to change when I mentioned one day that he would be better off working for someone else in the motor trade, doing the work he enjoyed still, but letting someone else do all the worrying over running a garage.

Within a few months he had made up his mind to move. He sold the garage, bought a house near a large garage not far away, in Stony Stratford, and became a motor mechanic there.

I still recall the day before they moved, I offered to help and was offered a cup of tea in the house while they took a break from packing. The wife said "I want to give you a little present". She got up and removed the electric clock from the wall and pulled out its plug. "Here, please take this and find a home for it. I never want to see it again. Every day we have been here Bert has never had enough hours to do the work of this place, and now he'll have as much time as he wants every week end and all the Summer evenings, and he will be a lot better off for it".

I took the little red-faced clock, and as I was to leave that ministry and area soon after, I took it to my next church, and hung it in their Church Lounge. Some twenty-five years later I went back to a meeting at that church, and there in that lounge, the red-faced clock still kept perfect time. I looked up and remembered the story behind it, and smiled that no one else in that church would ever know its history.

Chapter 11
COUNTRYSIDE DIFFERENCES

Country life is so very different to that of the town or city. Village folk, like farmers, are masters of doing things in their own patch. As a townie I would always shop for every need, but village folk would mend and make do. A bit of bailer twine or wire could fix most things, and they took pride in catering for all their own needs, from growing their own food, or knowing just who could supply them with eggs, a chicken, or who was just killing a pig. Many a time we opened our front door to find a cardboard box containing fruit, or vegetables, or even something for the dinner, or breakfast table; and you could never know who had left it.

Was it because they knew a Minister did not get much pay? And this one had four children to feed? No I don't think so. It was just a natural love for one's neighbour. If ever we needed anything we would have several people ready to advise us where to go to find what we wanted, and very often they would just say "Just leave it with me for a day or two" and sure enough the need would be met with no thought of taking repayment.

Our Neighbours the Meadow Ladies

Our Church and Manse was sited on the edge of the village and the kitchen window looked out onto the lane as it left up hill turning off for the village for Yardley Gobion. Across the lane we could see the farmer's field of cows, which was a constant reminder that we were in the country.

One day we noticed that the cows had got out of their field and were walking around in the lane where traffic would hurtle down the incline. With the aid of the phone book I rang the farmer to tell him about his cows. He speedily arrived on a tractor, and with the help of a little stick he drove them all back into the field.

Within the next few days this happened several times, and each time we phoned the farmer, and watched him come and put the cows back into their field.

The following Monday morning we were awakened by a cow bellowing, and looking out from our bedroom window we saw that the cows were out in the lane yet again. I was heading for the phone when Audrey stopped me. "Leave this to me" she called as she hastily dressed.

Within a minute or two she was outside, having furnished herself with a stick, holding it aloft in her right hand, she shouted in an authoritative manner. "Come on Bessie" and again "Back you go". "Daisy, come on this way". They all turned to look at her. Wack! "Rosy, get in that field." Wack! That was enough for them they started to move toward the gate. "Come on Buttercup!" Wack! "Get in there!"

One started to run to the gate, and the others all followed, nearly pushing her over in their rush. As they did so a car rounded the top of the lane, seeing a cow in the lane he hooted and started to apply his brakes. Audrey walked to the rear of the cow "Get a move on, slow coach;" she called "you'll get run over". The cow ran straight through the gate into the field. The motorist tooted and waved his thanks as if this was something they did together every day.

Audrey walked up to the gate, where the cows stood at a respectable distance. "And you just stay in that field" she shouted "and don't come out here again, understand? " She tied the gate up with bailer twine like a professional, and turned back to the house.

I stood in the kitchen open-mouthed "This is a side of your character I never knew existed" I told her.

"And you better watch out in future" she said "Now I know how it's done, you know what to expect". "Put that kettle on... Buttercup". I did so with a moo.

"How ever did you know all those cows by name?" I asked

"I didn't" she smiled "But they didn't know that, any more than you did. Anyway they were Church of England cows, must have been, they weren't christened in our church were they!"

Rosehip Week

After this we felt a little more like country folk, but there were always country surprises. One Friday the children returned from school with "Next week is Rosehip Week, can we go?" what was Rosehip Week and where were they going? People were so amazed that we did not know, that it was difficult to get them to tell us. Finally we learned that all the next week children were asked to spend as much of their spare time as possible collecting Rosehips from the hedgerows. They were paid a penny or two per pound, which helped pocket money, and the school probably got some new books or something out of it too.

The bags of Rosehips went away to the factory to be made into Rosehip Syrup, later to appear on the Chemist shop's shelf.

It was during that week that Audrey and the four children decided to go out to the field next door for half an hour before tea. I went to my study. About fifteen minutes later I happened to pass by our landing window and looked to see if I could see them picking Rosehips in that field. What I saw I could not understand at first. There was Audrey and the four children running toward the gate just below me, and running with all their might! Rosehips were falling from them and as I watched, one dropped the precious bag of collected rosehips, then I saw a large black shape trundling behind them, the farmer's bull!

The two eldest children were the first to leap over the gate, and shout encouragement to the others. The third eldest arrived at the gate to be unceremoniously hoisted over by her knickers. Smartly followed by Mum who was now carrying the smallest, who was almost thrown over the gate. Followed very speedily by Audrey who rolled over, legs waving wildly.

The beast that chased them was now pawing the ground and panting two or three feet away from the gate. I stopped to see no more, but hastened to greet the party at the front door. "You haven't got many Rosehips" I commented to which I was greeted by five loud accounts of their being chased for their lives. I looked at Audrey "And I thought you were so good with cows" I said "Cows! Cows!" They shouted! But it was the smallest little voice who explained "It wasn't a cow daddy, it was

a great big fiery bull, and it nearly ate us all up".
(A miracle escape?)

Troublesome Compost

When the apple season came round, the good
chapel folk made sure that we did not go without.
Mostly eating apples, we enjoyed the fruit and
trying to be good gardeners we also attempted to
store some for later enjoyment.

Sadly one box of apples did not take to storing
and Audrey asked me to throw them onto the
compost heap. Remembering the task during the
day I duly picked up the cardboard box from the
storehouse at the back of the house, and walked
through the house with it, across the chapel yard,
and right across the large garden at the back of the
church hall, to the compost heap. There I more
fully opened the top of the box and threw the
contents onto the heap. I was shocked and alarmed
to discover that the box had contained not only the
rotten apples but also there were two large rats
which fell with the apples onto the heap, and then
rushed about looking for somewhere to hide.

One came in my direction until I shouted and jumped about a bit. Finally they found shelter under some old bricks and stones right next to the compost heap. They were probably more frightened than I was, but the thought of my carrying two large live rats all that way in my arms was the stuff of future nightmares.

Having told Audrey, she came out, but there was nothing to see. She undertook to stay and watch, from a distance, to see if the rats came from their hiding place, while I slipped down the road to tell Mr Barby, one of the Deacons, who was only a few doors away.

Jim Barby heard my story calmly, and returned with me bringing with him his gun. I suspected that Jim enjoyed a tasty rabbit from time to time, now I was to learn that he kept down vermin with that gun too. "This may take a bit of time, and will require patience, and complete silence" Jim confided. "We won't see anything of those two rats until they are completely sure that there is no one about."

Audrey slipped away leaving us to it; she had better things to do! Jim and I just stood there some twenty or thirty feet away from the compost heap, and dare not take our eyes from the scene.

Lacking the staying power of country folk I was about to whisper that we might go for a coffee, when Jim very slowly brought his gun to his shoulder. I looked, and then I saw them, they remained quite still for probably a minute, then with a rush they were on top of the compost chewing at something.

A few seconds later Jim's gun exploded in a deafening bang. One rat lay dead, and the other was squealing on its back.

Like a shot Jim covered the ground to the compost heap and with the butt of his gun put the wounded rat out of its misery. Two dead rats lay before us. It was a good shot, and I was thankful to see that the vermin would not be in our house, or in anyone else's.

Digging up the Past

The Church was founded way back in 1690, it was square in shape, and as one sat in a pew looking to the front, it had the usual small platform with communion table, and the pulpit behind it.

However, to the left there was a square area with a piano (in case the organ on the right side failed) and beyond the piano a door leading to the Minister's Vestry, from which there was also another door leading to the Manse via a small court yard.

My wife decided to redecorate the Minister's Vestry which was a gloomy room, hung with pictures of past ministers. It was she who first noticed that the area on which the piano stood, looked somehow strange. The Church Secretary and myself looked hard at the area one Sunday, and decided that the floorboards were sagging under the weight of the piano. We moved the piano to a safer place, deciding that the supporting timbers underneath must be rotten and failing to support the floorboards.

Monday morning saw us taking up the floor, and when the floorboards were removed, and the whole area had been exposed, we could see that the timber joists were indeed rotted away.

Happily there was a village pub being demolished at the other end of the village, so we decided to see if we could obtain replacements from there. In the meantime I suggested that we clean up the rubbish that seemed to have accumulated on the site.

Armed with a wheelbarrow in the aisle, I applied a spade to the rubbish. There were lots of rotting wood, dust and bits of stone. Even a few bits of stale bread, evidence of visiting rats; or did I have rats on my brain? From about two feet below the church floor level, I started in with the spade and filled one barrow. Returning the empty barrow I got to work again with the spade.

Suddenly my spade came up with a human scull. To say that I was shocked was an understatement!

This meant that I was digging up human remains, so of course all work stopped at once.

Later, searching through the records we discovered that one of my predecessors had died in office, and had been buried 'Near the pulpit' some two hundred and fifty years earlier. As we looked at his picture in the vestry there was no mistaking the shape of his head.

With prayers for his continued rest in peace, we reverently replaced the skull, and left the site just as it was; we repaired the floor with the ex-pub joists and replaced the piano.

Returning to that church many years later I could not help looking at the place and wondering how many hundreds of years it might be before those boards might have to be replaced again and someone else would find what we had found. I feel sure that Our Lord will have returned again before then, so perhaps I need not worry that someone else will get a shock and dig up the past.

Chapter 12
OTHER VILLAGES

"Why does God send an Angel to some people, like Mary in the Christmas Story, but He never sends one to me?" The question came from someone only just in her teens, and she really wanted to know the answer I could see.

"God mostly works through people" I told her, "But there are times when God has to use an Angel because no human being could do the job that He wants done. In Mary's situation, no human being could tell her that she was to bear a son without the help of a man, and that God was to be the Father, and Jesus was going to be the most special person that ever walked the earth."

After a little more conversation, she comprehended the answer, and seemed satisfied.

Looking back, I wished I had also explained how God usually uses His own beloved ones to reach and help others, and that I had seen God use very ordinary little people like me to perform miracles in the lives of people. To me the following story illustrates the great lengths God will go just to touch another's life and bring Blessings.

Every Minister gets letters or phone calls from other churches from time to time asking if he will conduct worship in their church. A small church that cannot afford a Minister sometimes finds it hard to fill the pulpit every Sunday, and while there are many good lay-preachers, some people like to have a Minister to conduct worship, especially when The Holy Communion service is involved.

I received such an invitation one day from Haddon Congregational Church. Haddon was a village a few miles away. Several of my Deacons and members seemed to know something of the church and urged me to go, and as they only held an afternoon act of worship and I already had someone in mind who was available to take my afternoon service, I made the arrangement to go. I must say that at this stage I had no thought that

God might have something special for me as an outcome of the visit.

It was during that visit to conduct their service that they told me of a need. "We do our best to visit and keep in touch with our people". They explained "But some of our members have not had a Minister visit them for many years."

Of course I was busy with three churches and congregations to care for, but I found myself agreeing to have a list of their people and try to go and see some of them. I also undertook to take the occasional service at their church.

Soon after this I scheduled a Friday afternoon for visits in their village, and the third visit I made was to a widow called Mrs Field. All I knew of her was that she and her husband had been members and hard workers at the Haddon Church all their lives; and that now she was a widow.

I was somewhat taken aback when the door of the lovely old cottage was opened by a tall good looking young man, who invited me in, saying that he would call his mother. She entered the room dressed in out door clothes, saying that I had only just caught them, as they were just going out.

I offered to leave at once, but she would not hear of it. We chatted for a little before I reminded her of her plans to go out. She called her son, and they agreed not to go, wherever they were planning to go, and she introduced me to Clough.

Foolishly, I presumed that he was also a member of the church and chatted to him about God and our life of walking with Him as a Christian. During the conversation his mother left us to remove her outdoor clothes and make a pot of tea, and I chatted to Clough, who said little about himself and his Christian beliefs, but seemed to hang on my words with great interest and to ask many questions.

Time seemed to fly as we talked on about the Christian attitude to various aspects of life, I was given a full high tea, then it was cleared away and the conversation went on, sometimes with his mother present, sometimes not.

At last I had to leave, I had been there for hours. I had a prayer with them, and as I left I said "As it so happens I am taking the service here at your church this Sunday afternoon, so I look forward to seeing you both on Sunday."

I prayed that the visit might have been helpful, then forgot about it until I visited the church on Sunday afternoon, and there was Clough and his mother at the service.

I had no idea that this visit of Clough to church was making such a stir among the congregation. For what I did not know was that he had not been to church for years, and that his life now moved in high society with a rather upper class set, he ran a super red sports car, and was considered by the village to be a very much a non church, non religious, living it up sort of person.

The Church Secretary told me all this after the service was over, when everyone else had gone home, and we were alone in the vestry. "Now I HAVE seen a miracle". She said in wonderment!

As I drove home my mind was full of questions. Was Clough really so far from God as they suggested? If so why had he attended church? What ought I to do now? Of course the answer soon came, Talk to The Lord about it, and this I did. No voice came, but I was left with a certain conviction that God knew just what He was doing in all this and that I would be led to do whatever I was to do if He wanted me to do anything further, in the mean time I had two other services to conduct that day.

At lunchtime on Monday I found my thoughts back at the previous day's worship at Haddon, and felt a strong desire to go back to the village, perhaps I should visit some others that I had seen on Sunday.

As I drove there I became aware that any member of that church that I visited would surely say something about Cough's visit, and I would not know what to say, so I found myself driving to visit him and his mother.

They will probably be out I told myself, Clough would be at work I expect. What was I doing there?

Both Clough and his mother came to the door, they had seen me coming they said. I felt a bit guilty not knowing what to say, or what reception I would get.

Clough seemed to take charge, he asked his mother to get a cup of tea, and sat me in a comfortable chair, he then set about discussing my Sunday sermon, asking questions, and wanting backup from the Bible for certain points. The answers seemed to flow from me, and I later became convinced that it was God doing the talking rather than me. Which often happened!

Two cups of tea, a cake and a chocolate biscuit later we were in deep conversation about the things of living a Godly life, while his mother sat quietly listening. Suddenly their chiming clock awoke me to the fact that it was half-past five, and I was supposed to be home for tea at five and had an evening meeting. I left with haste, but I had ringing in my ears Cough's voice saying "How soon can you come again?"

Over the next few weeks I called on Clough as often as I could arrange it. When visiting late, his mother always sent me home with a hot water bottle in my heaterless car. Then came one evening when I stayed discussing the things of Christ till after midnight, and left with joy in my heart, for Clough had prayed and asked Jesus for forgiveness for all the past, and had asked Jesus to come into his life. Clough's life was completely changed from that moment on he became just a wise, happy man of God.

Before I left that area and Ministry I had the joyous task of receiving Clough into membership of Haddon Church. He had become a new man, and it showed! He still retained contact with his old friends but they accepted that now he was a Christian, they could see the change in his life and they respected him for it. He did go through some really tough temptations, but he learnt how to pray his way through them. He was a good example of Christian living to us all.

Later he asked if I could help him to become a lay preacher, and I was happy to help him in this way. He had his own personality shining through when he took services; his sermons were short but full of sincerity and truth. The little country churches soon loved to have him as their preacher, and more than once I was able to offer him my pulpit when I later had moved to a bigger church. As time went on he was also elected to be a Deacon at his own little church in Haddon, which just shows how much his Godliness shone through.

I have known him now for over thirty years, and his faith and Godly living has never diminished. He had to endure a crippling life which eventually made it difficult for him to even move around the cottage. His Mother died years ago, so he had to live all alone. He never married. Recently

I journeyed back to his village to attend his funeral which was one of joy, for another saint was safe in the arms of his Lord Jesus.

Although Clough knew that his salvation came from God and that I had nothing to do with it, accept be the messenger boy, he showed his love for me like a brother, and often thanked God for me because I had been the one chosen to show him God's truth. As I saw The Lord's love shine from him I also loved him like a brother.

After three and a half years as Minister to that group of country churches God showed me that I must move on. I was called to a church in Gloucestershire, and began to make plans to move. I did have one problem though.

I had come to that group of churches with a car, I had given it away when the group supplied a car for my use, now I would have to leave that group car behind, and I had no money at all to buy another to take to my new, rather large area. All I could do was to pray that God would solve the problem somehow.

A week or so before my move, Clough had told me that he had ordered a new car as the red sports car was no longer the sort of car he wanted, I think it reminded him too much of his old life! I was not surprised when he drove into my churchyard to show me his new car, a small blue saloon. I was surprised when he asked me to stay in for the rest of the afternoon, and obtained a promise from me that I would not go out.

Soon after Clough drove away another car drove in to the yard, and yet another was standing at the gate. A gentleman got out and came to my door "I am just delivering your car, sir" the gentleman said "Would you please come and check it over before I leave it?" although the man would not say who had given me this car, I knew it was Clough. I looked around, sat in, and rejoiced in this gift of a smart shiny green Morris Mini Traveller, only two years old and the perfect answer to my prayers.

The man was whisked away back to his garage in the car at the gate, and I was left to gaze at my new acquisition, and praise The Lord for it. As soon as I got to Cough's cottage I poured out my thanks. In a quiet voice he simply said "Don't spoil it my friend, The Lord told me to do it, and we both know who it really comes from, it comes from our mutual friend and Master."

For several years Clough drove that new blue car of his over to my new church and shared Sunday Worship with Audrey and I, and of course my family. All through these years we have phoned one another and shared a wonderful friendship. Once he became housebound his preaching days were over, but we still let brotherly love continue and just occasionally I visited him. Never in all that time have I heard him complain about his painful disability, or anything else.

In all his years he could never understand about things electrical or mechanical. On the rare occasion that his car broke down he would just get out of it, look helpless, and offer a prayer for help. Every time someone would come along and fix the problem for him and send him on his way.

When he had his sports car someone told him that it was a good thing, once he had put it into his garage, to put a blanket over the bonnet to keep the engine right, so this was what he always did. However when he got his new little blue car I noticed that he still put a blanket over the front end. "Why do you do that" I asked. He explained that he did it to keep the engine warm. I said "didn't you know that your new car has its engine at the rear, the front is for luggage."

"Oh, I suppose it is" he replied "I remember now they did say that, when I bought it. I've never opened either end since I bought it."

We often had a good laugh over this, and as the blanket kept sliding off the rear engine end he never put it on the car at all after that. A brilliant mind for other things, but in such mechanical or electrical items he just seemed lost. Happily he had many friends and there was always someone who would mend a fuse, or put water in his radiator. And they loved to do it for him.

Chapter 13
TIME TO GO

I have mentioned that I eventually left the country ministry and how a car wonderfully came my way. I must say that I look back on that time with those country churches with feelings of pleasure, although it did have its sad occasions. Even in such a quiet and delightful area Satan could be seen at work from time to time.

There was the time when I had succeeded in getting the young people together in a happy fellowship, and they were almost ready to make their profession of faith in Christ. We were going on well together; they enjoyed all the activity, and were receiving Christian teaching in one happy fellowship. Then suddenly they were absent. They did not turn up for social or spiritual events, and to my surprise they were even missing at Sunday worship and Sunday School, and most of them had been coming from a very early age.

As I went to their homes to enquire about this I was told by the parents that the C of E vicar had called on them all, and reminded them that they must all attend Confirmation Classes and be confirmed. This they now dutifully did, and in due course they were Confirmed as members of the Church of England. I had no problem with this, but after this they neither attended the Parish Church or the Congregational Church. When I spoke to the parents and the young people about this I got the same answer "Now we have been confirmed we don't have to go to church anymore, we are Christians!"

This came as a heartbreak for me, they would slowly get lost to God in the worldliness of everyday living. Without the care and fellowship of a group of God's people, over time they would become easier prey to temptations, and, rejecting the contacts with their creator God they would fall away from the Kingdom of God. Deep inside, I wept! For I loved them. Yes, there were heartbreaks even in this nice country Ministry.

As a Minister I have never found it easy to leave one church and go to another. The final Act of worship is always sad for both Minister and people. There are those who have found God's Blessings and Healing together with their man of God: For some there has been a sharing of a marriage, or other happy events with him: There are the times when sorrow or bereavement has been shared: And there are always good friendships that face the parting. No, the parting of a Minister to another church is never a happy time.

What makes a Minister leave one church and go to another? I suppose that this must differ from one man to another, for I have known of some Ministers who remain in the one church all their life, or for very many years. I think it all depends on the work that God gives a Minister to do, and on the talents or abilities The Lord has supplied.

Looking back over my life and Ministry I think God made me a kind of 'trouble shooter' within His Church. I have been called to churches that have a problem, or are going through a difficult patch, and by The Grace of God I have been led to steer those churches back to a steady path before I left them.

I have always found the change from one church to another has a two-fold challenge. God calls one away from the church that you are serving, and then also shows you where you are to go and gives unmistakable orders. It happened so now that I was moving away from this lovely country group of churches.

The Group of these three churches had been an experimental one from the start, and after three years I became aware that the income from the people was not enough to maintain a Minister and church. As Congregational Churches are all independent, there is no organisation or denominational body with funds or help. If the church members cannot afford to pay for the upkeep of buildings or the maintenance of a Minister they have to do without, or raise what is needed. I was aware that I was going to be a real burden on these little churches in the not too distant future. New members had only replaced those who were no longer with us, and while costs went up, income did not.

I also felt that I had poured out my all to these lovely people and that I had not much more that I could give. I had managed to get the great London

Emanuel Choir to come from London and give a wonderful weekend. I had also obtained the current Christian Pop Group 'The Peacemakers' and packed the village hall with young people to hear them. I had used the then popular film Ministry, but there was no great outcome to these efforts to interest the village folk in taking an interest in God or the church. I was feeling now that I could do little more in this Ministry. This was the call away from this work for me. God was going to move me on!

Chapter 14

GOD MOVES IN STRANGE WAYS

Quite out of the blue I had a phone call from the Moderator, who had a problem to share with me, and this is the story he unfolded:

"I have a church that I would like to tell you about, Gerald. It is right in the centre of a small town, well established over many years, with a fine record. They have had a young Minister who has suddenly left them, in fact, he has left the Ministry. The circumstances of his going have caused a great deal of upset in the church, so much so, that they have taken the decision to close the church."

"This is something that they realise cannot be done quickly, and they want to settle the people in other churches in the town before closure. I have spent time at both their Deacons and Church Meetings trying to help them, and I have got them to agree to consider having another Minister, even if only until the church is closed."

"I have spent much time in prayer about this distressing situation, and I am convinced that you are the man that God is leading me to talk to about it. Just consider, if you will; the churches where you are now, can no longer sustain a Minister and you ought to be thinking of moving soon. I am aware of what you have done in the three and a half years you have been there, and in my opinion, and the opinion of the deacons of all three churches, you have done a fine job."

"This church I am telling you about may not invite you, and you may not feel led to go anyway. But I am asking you to consider visiting them to conduct a Sunday Worship, and talk to them, and just see where it might lead."

That was his message, and I agreed to pray and think over what he had said, and to contact him again with my decision. A colleague of mine who had been in college with me, had Ministered in a new church with brand new church buildings and every facility one could wish for, and I had wondered whether The Lord might call me to such a church; this proposal from the Moderator was just about the reverse of everything I could dream of, but I prayed about it and discussed it with Audrey.

The result of all my heart-searching was to at least go and visit the church. There was only one doubt in my mind, it did not seem fair to my present churches that I should have a Sunday off to go to another church, and it did not seem right to make such a journey in the car supplied by these churches.

I shared the pulpit problem with each church secretary in turn and their answers were all the same, "I know of a lay preacher I can get to take a Sunday, you go!" Clough, my good friend from the Haddon Church came over to see me and I shared the news with him. To my amazement, without him knowing my fears about using the Group Car, he suggested that I borrow his car for the journey, jokingly saying "If you go in my red sports car they will think you are a young modern parson and won't call you at all, then you will stay here with us!"

I phoned the Secretary of the church and made a date to visit the church one Saturday and return after the Sunday worship. I phoned the Moderator who seemed very pleased that I was taking that first step in what he obviously thought would be that church's solution. I bravely said to God "I am not looking forward to this, and I don't really want to go, but You and I have a contract, and it is Your Will that shall be done."

I drove to the church through some of the most beautiful country side I had ever seen, all decked in glorious autumn colours, and arrived at the church just as crowds of church people were clearing up after running their annual bazaar. It wasn't the best time to be introduced to loads of new names and new faces, all tired and busy.

As I recall it, I attended a special meeting of Deacons in the evening, they asked the usual questions about me, and I tried to find out what I could about the church and their problem. It seemed that their previous Minister had been reading a book written by a then popular bishop, and it had changed his views on the Bible and God. He had made the statement one Sunday to the whole church to the effect that he could no longer hold to the Christian Faith as most people saw it, and that he would eventually leave the church altogether.

In the uproar that this caused, he was stopped from preaching at once, and removed from the Ministry altogether. But as far as the people were concerned there was great upset and consternation.

As I spoke to people both on Saturday and Sunday I realised that the faith of many had been weakened or upset. How could they see this man as a Man of God when they called him to be their Minister and now face the fact that he denied God and the Gospel?

The big question for me was How strong was the decision to close the church? As I spoke to one and another they were presuming that the closure was coming, but I detected sadness at the prospect, and a spirit of regret.

I returned home in Cough's sports car with much to think about and pray over. I had spoken very plainly to the Deacons, and felt very warm feelings toward the people, after much thought I just had to turn it over to God and wait for some leading.

The first part of the leading came by way of a phone call from the Church Secretary. He was cautious, saying that this was an unofficial call, just to know what I had thought following my visit.

After a bit of verbal sparring, he asked what my reaction might be IF the church considered giving me a call to be their Minister. My answer came almost without me thinking about what I was saying. A sign of The Holy Spirit's leading, I thought afterwards.

"If the church was led to call me I would expect that such a decision was led by The Holy Spirit, and nothing less. Such a call would have to be the unanimous vote of the whole membership, and it would have to be on the clear understanding that the church would work with me to build for a future, rather than have a negative attitude of closing. I would not be prepared to consider coming to prepare for the funeral service of their church."

There was a silence after this statement, it lasted so long that I wondered what he was thinking and what he would reply. Then slowly he read back the statement I had made and I realised that he had been busy writing it down. I too scribbled a quick note of the statement for my own use, and I remembered correcting one little bit, and telling him that what I had said had come just as I had spoken and had not been a prepared statement.

"When people speak at Church Meetings, with sorrow, anger, or strong feelings," I told him "They are apt to say things in haste, which they find difficult to retract later on sober reflection".

"I suspect that something like this may have happened in your church, but we must all remember that we are here to serve the Risen Christ, not our own desires. My advice is that the church should be much in prayer for The Will of God, and believe that He will show it to them".

Over the next few weeks there were phone calls from the church to the Moderator, and from the Moderator to me. I remained in the attitude of "Lord I shall have no tears if I am not called to this church, I still don't really want to go, but You know best, so I just wait to know what You want me to do. But Lord I would much rather be called to a nice big church, especially a nice newly built one."

Then came the letter from the church. "The Deacons and Church had spent time in prayer, and had met in a Special Church Meeting to discuss the church affairs. A resolution was passed unanimously (one elder lady abstaining as she did not know enough about the matter to vote), That the church call me to be their full-time Minister, on the understanding that although some still thought the church should close, all were pledged to try to build for the future and back the new Minister in every effort to give the church a hoped for happy future."

Once The Lord had convinced me that I should accept, Audrey and I made several furthers contacts and visits to the new church and area. They had to buy another house for us to live in, and we had to make inquiries about schooling for the children, but it was obvious from the first that this was where God was calling us to be, and all the problems fell away in solutions, even our transport problem!

So, finally we were there in an area that was outstanding in beauty, the people seemed very friendly and helpful, and I soon felt happy to be there. But there were a few people who were obviously pessimistic about the church's future. The Church Treasurer, who was a pleasant man most of the time, was constantly telling me that he "did not know where my stipend was coming from this month". A few members slipped off to some other church from time to time because they would have to go there when the church closed. There were one or two who just could not wait for the end of my first year of Ministry so that they could get on with the church resolution to close up.

There were two Deacons who blocked any spending of money on the desperate needs for work to be done on the church buildings. "There is no sense in spending money on a building that will not be here in a year's time" was their attitude. There were people who were still asking serious questions about the things of our faith, resulting from the obvious doubts that had been put into their minds over the crisis concerning the past minister. As a Bible based man I had the answers, but it always seemed to involve much discussion.

At last my first year came to an end and I rather dreaded the Deacon's Meeting that was sure to bring problems. There were three Deacons who were determined to have the church closed, and I was not sure how the other nine would react. Even as I opened the meeting I felt the opposition.

As I suspected, the three had everything ready and planned. Their argument was just this:-

We have given the requested year since the decision of the church was taken to close. Nothing had changed since that decision was taken and we must now put that proposal into action, and as quickly as possible. They quoted the numbers of church members and adherents, also the number of children in the Sunday School. They named the churches in the town that were keen to welcome these people into their fellowships, they even named people and where they were going.

I wondered about their motives as they went on to say that the church would sell easily as it was on a prime site in the centre of town, and it would only be right that the income from the sale should be distributed among the churches that were opening their doors to receive and welcome us.

The speech was ended by a resolution to The Church Meeting from their Deaconate "That the Church close as soon as possible". It was speedily and enthusiastically seconded by the second of the three, and the third said briefly how much the whole church should be thankful to the Minister for the noble way he had fought to save the dying church.

There followed one or two who considered that it was wrong to sell the church, that there was still hope of saving it, that we should give it more time. They were argued against by pleas to look facts in the face, the buildings were old and in great need of repair, there was no hope of raising the money for all that had to be done. People would soon be happily settled in other churches and those churches in turn would be strengthened. Finally the motion was carried. I rose to my feet and told them that since the church was to close, and I was not needed to build the church up for its future greatness, I resigned as their Minister, asking that the church continue to let me Minister until I could see where God would call me, and I could move to another work.

I went home with tears in my heart, and crying to God for guidance and understanding.

Chapter 15

GOD KNOWS WHEN WE ARE DOWN

I was still on my knees in the study when the front door bell rang. It was one of our younger Deacons who I knew was keen to see the church remain open. He took me by the hand. "What was done tonight was wrong" he said "I want you to know I am with you if you will stay and rebuild this as a church for the future."

Even as he spoke the doorbell rang again, Audrey showed in a second Deacon. "Please don't leave us" his face was earnest "If you will stay I'll be with you to build the church up again."

The bell rang again and in came two other Deacons; they looked surprised to see the other two "Are you here to support our church in the future" one asked? While they were being answered the bell went yet again, and we ended up with seven

Deacons, and I was told of one more who was with them, but could not get to The Manse.

As I recall, we spent quite a time in prayer together, and left with greater hope for the future. I awaited the Church Meeting with loathing, I hate disunity in people, and I could well imagine some very heated discussion, and as chairman I was to be in the middle.

When it came the proposal was put from the Deacons Meeting that the church close. Then one after another eight of the Deacons rose to withdraw their support from the proposal, with exciting hopes for the church's future. This aroused the opposition to plead their facts and figures and the logic of closure. The Church Members were plainly torn between the arguments.

I stood to tell the confused meeting that I had come as their Minister on the unanimous decision and agreement that the church was going to work with me to build the church up for the future. That pledge has not been honoured! Money for essential repairs has been withheld because "you will close". Some have even visited other churches to warm a seat there for the future. In fifty years time this church could still be here as a witness to your faith in the spread of the gospel in this town, though you and I won't be here to see it, but we can still enjoy it in the meantime. This decision to close or stay open should have been settled before you called me, I thought it was!

To quote Elijah "How long will you halt between two opinions", if The Lord is God, together with Him we will build, if not, if there is no faith ... you had better vote to close the church.

There was silence as I sat down. I thought that no one was going to say anything. Then a little old lady stood up at the back of the meeting. "The Minister better know that I was the one who abstained from voting for him to come as Minister. Well, I am voting for him now, he has only been here a year and I can see the difference in peoples' hearts, and that is where it counts!" She was finding it difficult to say what she wanted to say "Our church had taken quite a fall, but when you fall, you don't just lie there, you GET UP, you dust yourself down, and start all over again. I had better sit down" she said, sitting "If I don't, I shall fall down." To my surprise this was greeted with applause!

The little elderly Deacon, who had been unable to attend at the Manse, now rose to his feet. He had much sympathy with the members as both he and his wife had suffered much illness recently. "Perhaps the members will not know this" he sadly said "But our Minister tendered his resignation at the Deacons Meeting and is probably already looking for another church. This meeting had better remember that it will face God Himself with the decisions it makes tonight. It could mean that we lose a good Minister, a once happy, and can be again, happy fellowship, it stands to lose forever a church standing in a centre of town, and the Manse! And for what? A seat in some other church! All our money and all we have worked so hard for to keep our church will go, not to You, but to some other churches. Why! I ask? When we could start all over again. We were married in this church, so were some of you, we have all had some good times and spiritual blessings here. It can be so again".

Speeches like this turned the tide, although the opposition worked hard to put their side. Finally it was decided to forget any idea of closure and review the matter in another year. The Minister withdrew his resignation!

One year later, at a Deacons Meeting, the secretary was asked to put the item on the agenda, and when it came the three opposing Deacons stated that they could see no sign of great change in the church and therefore proposed that the church should return to the work of closing the church.

They repeated the augments of the previous year. The matter was quickly seconded and the discussion started. Now the other Deacons were all for building up the church and forgetting any idea of closure permanently.

The opposing three became hot and bothered repeating their case for closure. I called a halt to the proceedings and said that we would have a brief time of quiet prayer, asking God for a unity and preparedness for us all to now work together for the work of The Kingdom here in our church.

The eldest in opposition rose to his feet, his face red with anger, his chair falling over behind him. "That is just the way you would try to get your own way" he exploded "Well you are going to need your prayers when this church falls apart and has to close anyway." He started to put on his overcoat "I resign from this Deaconate, and from this church, and like a good many more, I shall never enter this place again as long as I live!" He stormed out.

The other two now also stood, one said "That goes for me too". And he started to put on his coat. The other said "I am sorry that our friend lost his temper, but you can understand why, we all feel that you are wrong to try to stay open, and I think you will have to close sooner or later, but although I resign from this church, I wish you well, and harbour no grudge".

We heard their footsteps going down the stairs, we felt sad, and I felt also a feeling of relief. I led them in prayer, and we resumed the agenda, and soon we were happily laughing and pulling one another's legs. I somehow felt that we were making a new start and that the future looked bright.

Looking back now over thirty years, I was to stay with them for just over seven years and to set that church on to a very good future. The Church is still there, and great things have happened since that great struggle to keep it open. The man of God who followed me had a long and fruitful ministry and was dearly loved and respected, he also became President of The Congregational Federation for a year, and died a few years later still in office. Today the church is still standing, although like many churches in this now pagan land numbers have gone down. I receive their Church Magazine every month and the people are still in good heart.

Sending a Rocket to Mars

My time at this church was certainly not without problems and troubles. Soon after the settling down to rebuild the church, we had trouble with the roof. For several Sundays we held services with buckets standing in the aisle to catch the rainwater that was leaking through.

The experts were called in and the news was not good, it was a very large roof and very high up; we would have to spend several thousand pounds more than we had. The temptation to wonder if those departing Deacons had been right in their gloomy picture of our future was always there. We believed that we had been right to keep the church open, so with faith in God we turned to prayer.

While waiting upon The Lord one morning the answer came. We needed something that would catch the imagination and keep peoples attention on the urgent need over a period that it would take to raise the money. Here was the scheme.

The world news at that time was very much centred on sending rockets into space and the moon.

We would launch a "Rocket to Mars"! The Church agreed to my idea, and I asked Bill Knight, one of our Deacons to build a Rocket of cardboard that could be lifted from the stage in the hall until it was out of sight above the stage curtains. He did a grand job of it too, standing about six foot tall and painted just like a real rocket.

We set a special evening aside to launch the rocket, and with the aid of the local press I advertised that people could "send a message to Mars" for a donation to the roof fund. Not only Church Members but also a number of friends in the district happily gave a donation and wrote their message to Mars. Many of the messages turned out to be prayers for a new roof.

The day of the launch came and many bought tickets for the launching ceremony. It was an evening of entertainment with refreshments. It concluded with the Countdown when everyone counted. "10.. 9..8.. 7.. 6.. 5.. 4.. 3..2.. 1 Lift off."

With a blinding flash and clouds of smoke the rocket rose straight up and disappeared, to loud applause.

During the weeks that followed the progress of the rocket was shown as more donations and efforts pushed the graph ever upward. At last we were able to report that The Rocket had landed. The scaffolding went up outside the church and the workmen started the essential roof work. We were soon offering thanks to God for what seemed to us a miracle.

During the first three years of this ministry the church was living from hand to mouth. As fast as we added new members, I was conducting funerals of elderly faithful members and this kept the membership figures at the same level. Happily, we did start to grow, and the blessings did start to come.

We created two new and much needed toilets on the ground level, knocked down an old disused building at the back and built there a small car park. Also we started improvements to the kitchen. The Church was growing. Outsiders came to our weekly Coffee Morning in the hall. The Bible

Study weekly event became quite popular. Prayer and hope in the future were coming to fruition.

The house (Manse) that the church obtained for us to live in had a wonderful neighbour living opposite us. Many will know his name, Rev: Wilbert Awdry, or The Thomas The Tank Engine writer. We became good friends, and of course shared a love for the World wide hobby of Model Railways.

I was still a beginner in the hobby then, and one day I asked him for his advice. I had foolishly not studied the subject, and had made endless mistakes. I told him that I had rolling stock from every region and did not want to buy all new and start again.

He suggested that I do what he had done, he had invented the island of Sodar so that he could run whatever stock he wanted, and there would be no criticism that it did not fit with a particular region. I took his advice and invented an island called St Francis Island, and so began the St Francis Island Railway. I mapped it all out with mountain range, towns, and the railway which runs to a proper time table, and sound.

It has appeared in Model Railway Magazines, on film and on BBC television, peak viewing time Christmas Eve. And it has relaxed me whenever I over work, and been an enjoyment through my busy life. A real Blessing, if not a miracle.

Chapter 16
A BUS AT CHRISTMAS TIME

I suppose it might be something to do with my childhood experiences, but Christmas has always been a magic, thrilling time, and each year it usually started with hearing choirs singing carols around the streets. Most churches had choirs who went out singing at this joyous time of year, so everyone heard lots of good quality harmonious singing of the Christmas message by people who were singing, not for money, but for the happy sharing of the Gospel message in which they believed. How sad that now we only get two or three small children ringing our door bells singing just a chorus of "We wish you a merry Christmas" with a desire to collect money. This year I offered the only set of children who called, fifty pence, if they would sing one verse of "Away in a manger" and they could not remember the words.

My mind goes back to 1970 when I was chairman of a welfare committee who were endeavouring to raise some money to give much needed food, clothing and toys to poor families in the district. Especially at Christmas time.

To get such money is never easy, for it is essential to ask people, and explain the need, and this means some form of advertising, which in turn would cost money.

It was at this time that I put forward a suggestion, based on what I had seen done elsewhere. If I could get the help I needed I would use a van or motor lorry, mounted with a generator to supply electricity, and tour the streets with recorded Christmas Carols, collecting money for the needy. I showed drawings of what I had in mind, and told of the firms that might loan the equipment.

Sadly the committee did not think it could be done, so the matter was dropped.

Happily I shared the idea with one of my Church Deacons, who was a bus driver, and he took the idea away to think about it and then he shared it with the men at his bus garage. They became enthusiastic over my idea and started to think in terms of a bus instead of a lorry.

Eventually I was invited to a meeting of the Bristol Omnibus Employees Welfare Club, where we discussed and planned how we might have a bus with a generator inside, powering not only sound equipment but coloured lights as well. The outside of the bus would be covered and painted to look like a castle, with some Christmas wish to all.

My task in all this would be to supply the Christmas Carols, and with a microphone wish everyone a Happy Christmas from time to time. It was also part of the plan to have Father Christmas sitting in an open-top car travelling behind the bus so that the children could wave to him. The Welfare Club undertook to run the bus side and if possible bear the cost and the manpower.

The idea caught the imagination and enthusiasm of the whole bus depot, and when the plans came to the bus company authorities they happily put their weight behind the project, and came up with the suggestion that the Tree Lopping Bus, an open-top bus parked at the garage, could be used. This meant that Father Christmas could wave from the top deck in the front of the bus, and I came up with the plan to have a choir sitting on the top deck singing carols, with some amplification.

As the weeks before Christmas came round the plans turned to work. The Stroud staff of the Bus Company were wonderful. They covered the Open-top Tree Lopping Bus with material and started painting it to look just like a castle. Added to this were holly and three hundred coloured light bulbs, plus loads of cotton wool snow. On the bonnet of the bus they built a sleigh and reindeer that might well have come straight out of Walt Disney, and when it was all finished it really did look a picture.

Meanwhile a generator had been fitted inside to provide electrical power, and on the top deck power plugs for me to plug in tape recorders and an amplifier. Microphones were fixed in at various points to pick up the voices of the choir.

Within the Bus Canteen lists were rapidly filled in of men and their wives who would go door to door collecting for charity. Collecting Tins were provided and proper collector authorisation labels were issued each night to the collectors. I contacted the police and obtained authorisation, and visited the local newspaper asking them to publish the days and times that the bus would visit the various parts of the district. They were very sceptical at first, but after it was launched they became wildly enthusiastic.

I did not find it very easy to arrange for a different choir to occupy the bus each night over the ten nights we planned to tour the district. As the idea was new and unheard of, and the people in each church were busy on different nights, it involved many phone calls, but at last I managed to book a different church choir for each night.

I also had the job of supplying hymn books and /or carol sheets with music for unknown numbers of choir members with different traditions. Although Christmas Carols are universal, it surprised me to find that many hymns books had different harmony, one to another, and in the early days I sometimes got the remark that the choir was not used to that or this harmony, but there was good humour and understanding and all went well.

I remember well the first night we went out for our Carol Bus trip. We met in the bus garage, and I had asked that the bus engine not be started until I had all the choir settled and had the opportunity to tell them what was going to happen. Crowds of collectors had gathered, all wrapped up warm, issued with their authorisation labels and collecting tins. I got the choir to stand in a group until all had arrived, then they were boarded onto the open top deck.

Father Christmas was to occupy the very front, with me just behind him facing the choir. There was also a small electronic organ, and the church organists were happy to come and play.

I arranged the choir into Basses and Tenors at the back seats and the rest in front of me, and explained one or two safety rules, then how I would run the rest of the trip, and how I would conduct when singing the carols so that we would all sing together.

With just three minutes to starting time I gave the all clear to start. There was one man in charge of the bus, one engineer in charge of the generator, and the driver on the lower deck and me to look after the top deck. Plus Father Christmas, who now joined us. The bus motor started up, the generator roared into life, and with the ring of the conductors' bell we moved off. Out of the shed and into the cold night air with three hundred coloured lights a blazing. As we turned into the road the first

Recorded Christmas Carol, sounded fortissimo through the speakers mounted front and back.

A tingle of pleasure ran through my body as slowly we moved with the army of collectors calling on the houses each side of the road.

As we approached the town centre I asked the choir to find our first carol, and alerted the organist. The recorded carol came neatly to a close as we approached a small party of local dignitaries who had come to cheer us on. Switching to the microphone I wished "A very Happy Christmas" and announced the name of the choir and what they would now sing. Switching over to the choir microphone system, the organist played the introduction and I brought the choir in. It could not have gone over better. The bus stopped for a couple of verses, and I left them singing to go down, partly to see what the effect was, and of course to thank the mayor and his party for coming to see us off. They all said that they were very impressed, and I was to thank all concerned.

For two hours we toured one part of the district, as planned and then returned, tired but happy that all had gone so well. As I saw the choir off the bus, I was thanked for letting them share in such a wonderful evening, and I heard the collectors happily talking about certain little children who had been "so sweet", and of good comments from people, and how happy they had been collecting. It was no easy task to mount flights of steps, journey up garden paths and cover blocks of flats, but they tried not to miss anyone with their collecting tins, and these came back very heavy.

Everyone had worked so hard on what was an unknown project, and now felt that all their efforts had been well worthwhile. Long after the bus had been put to bed, independent witnesses gathered to watch the opening of the tins and the counting of the money. On the first night we had collected £45, which was very good indeed considering this was 1970, making the value much more than that sum today. This was immediately banked in the special account opened for the purpose. The next morning I had a phone call from the local newspaper saying that they had been inundated with messages of appreciation and enquiries for information. I agreed to them coming to the garage to take a photograph of the bus.

On the second night, Friday, I had the happy task of repeating the performance with a different choir and touring a different part of the district, it was cold, but I didn't hear one complaint. I had learnt lessons from the previous night, one of which was to be very careful to turn off the choir microphones as soon as a carol had been sung, as the choirs seemed to chat and laugh quite a bit when they were not singing and this could come through to the public.

The word had got around that we were coming and when we came to one part we discovered a sizeable crowd gathered on a large grass area. After we had stood there and sung one carol I asked the man in charge if we might stay for a few minutes. I lowered the microphone over the side of the bus, and with it I went among the crowds. Collecting together a group of small children I got them to sing "Away in a Manger". I then asked who might be the oldest lady in the crowd, I had her come forward and wish everyone "A happy Christmas" and asked her for her favourite carol, which, returning to the top deck I got the choir to sing.

There was such a warmth of spirit among the crowd as we departed the site with loudspeaker good wishes naming the old lady and the children. Somehow this intimate contact with people seemed to develop into a pattern for the future trips around the district. I knew several invalid people and would visit them before we were to travel past their house. As we drove past I would give them a special greeting and play or sing their requested carol. It became a common sight to see wheelchairs by front doors or in the street, and after a while the collectors joined in the idea, sometimes coming up to the top deck to tell me of some little child or other person who was sick, or who had some need and I would send them greetings from Father Christmas and all those on the bus.

That second night we had collected £54. On Monday it was £40. And so the ten-day tour of our district went on making many people very happy, and collecting £621/17/4d.

The local newspaper asked all local charities who wished to benefit from the gifts collected to apply, and the committee allocated gifts as seemed best.

The following year the Bus Company and workers agreed to have the Carol Bus again and the work was selflessly given all over again. I advertised in the paper that if any school in the district would like me to, I would visit their school with a tape-recorder and record their children singing a carol that would later be broadcast from the Carol Bus. Several Heads of school phoned me and I duly visited their schools.

Keen to get the best, I insisted that the children rehearsed, and got them to sing so that I got a high standard on the recording. I also made sure that I knew which piece came from which school so that I could give credit to the school when announcing it.

The 1971 tour included two rainy nights, which I thought might spoil things, but I was happily surprised to find the choir and collectors pleased to carry on armed with umbrellas.

According to my records The Carol Bus was received with as much enthusiasm as in the previous year, and we beat our previous year's collections with a £684 total.

While the Bus Company Employees were extremely generous in time, work and money, the Christmas Carol Bus was not cheap to run, and the Welfare Club had born all the cost so that nothing was taken from the collections for charity. It was a situation that could not continue year after year without some of the cost being taken from the money collected, so, as a committee we had to make the decision to use some of the money collected to pay some of the bills. It was a good job we did, for, little did we realise it then, but the regular Carol Bus was to go on year after year, long after I had left the district. It was a sad day when I was asked to travel back to the area over twenty-five years later to officially end the Christmas Carol Bus.

It must have given a great deal of pleasure to very many people over the years that it served the district, and a large number of people must have been helped through the generosity of ordinary people who gave their money, and so much hard work, like the people at the bus company and the churches. We shall never know just what good was done. But it also gave satisfaction and pleasure to those who made it all possible.

With so much pleasure given over all those years, with the yearly reminder of the first coming of Christ into this world, with such encouragement of good will and love, and with so much opportunity for people to be generous, and the help they gave to the poor and needy, who dares to say that this was not a miracle of God's good Grace. I count this as a bus size miracle.

Chapter 17

IT HAPPENED IN CHURCH ONE DAY

It was a very ordinary Sunday evening, and as I entered the pulpit to conduct worship my eye fell upon a middle-aged couple and a very attractive young lady sitting in one of the side pews to my left. The couple's faces were so familiar to me that even while I was leading the worship I was trying to remember who they were. But I just could not remember. The young woman was quite unknown to me I felt sure.

All through the service I kept trying to recall where I had seen them, so when the service was over I made my way to them to greet them. As soon as they reminded me of their name I recalled not only them but also their story.

The couple had been members of the church where I had been previously the Minister; I had joined them together in Christian Marriage, and shared the joy of their first expected child. But things had gone wrong when the baby was born.

I remembered how the husband had phoned me to say that his wife was all right but the baby girl had something wrong, and was not expected to live. This kind of statement, while reasonable as a warning to such parents did also leave a negative attitude, a feeling of despair that the outcome was hopeless.

I said that I would come to the hospital at once, but he asked if I could contact the hospital and arrange for me to baptise the little one at once, as the baby was not expected to live long, and this was something they both wanted.

This was not a time to discuss the importance of Baptism, but to just do what they asked. I duly phoned the hospital and spoke to one of the senior nurses. It was confirmed that they did not expect the child to live long, perhaps a day or two, and so a time was arranged for me to come for a service of Baptism with both parents present.

I remember that when I arrived at the hospital the father met me and we both had to dress up in white gowns before entering the private room set-aside for the purpose.

We had a little time talking about what we were going to do; we had a time of prayer, which was largely of thanksgiving for the Mother's life spared and for God's Blessing upon the situation. I then took the little baby in my arms and made the sign of the cross on her tiny forehead, Baptising her in the name of The Father, The Son, and The Holy Spirit. There was a very brief pause, and then I found myself praying for the baby by her new name. I cannot remember what I said, but I was aware that I was saying words that came to me, which in a strange way I was not thinking.

Later the child's father told me that I had asked the child's Great Heavenly Father to give new life and healing to this new life, and was thanking Him for this gift that would bring happiness to these two Christian Parents.

From that moment on the baby started to be just like any healthy child, she grew stronger, and mother and baby were back home within three weeks, with no sign of any trouble.

Introducing me now to the pretty young lady, these parents said "And this is that baby daughter, having now reached her twenty-first birthday". She gave me a kiss saying "I don't remember any of this of course, but as part of my twenty-first birthday celebrations, I wanted to thank you for what you did; I just wanted to come to church and see you, worship with you and to thank you". They came back to our house for supper and fellowship, after which they drove away, and I never saw them again.

When God wants to perform a miracle He seems to just get on with it... in spite of us.

At the top of the town there was another Congregational Church, we might call it The Old Chapel, for it was certainly that. It had a grand history stretching out behind it; in fact it was by far the oldest in the district. The early Independent Congregations worked and prayed to bring it into being, The Lord Himself alone knows just how much sheer sacrifice went into building it, people were very poor in those days.

It had its great Ministers, and packed congregations Sunday by Sunday. Masses of children started their Sunday School education there, the only education they ever got in those early days.

There was the story that on very special occasions when the church was so packed with worshippers, they had been known to take out the window behind the pulpit and seat crowds of people on the grass mound behind the church so that they also could join in the worship.

Such a church was the centre of community life all through the generations. It not only catered for the spiritual needs but for the educational and social needs too. Cricket, football, tennis, dramatics, socials, and meetings were all part of the church life for almost everyone in the top of town.

The plaques on the walls spoke of the people who had given their service, and passed on to their reward. The library of music gave testimony to the large choirs and the music festivals.

The massive building once was the soul and centre of the many living around it. Now it was very old and decaying. The people had largely moved away from this part of the town, and those who were around followed the trend to be secular and of godless spirit.

The church of which I was Minister was right in the centre of the busy shopping area and where the people were, but this Old Chapel had been its founder, and in those far off days sent down some of their crowds to form the church where I was now, we owed our being to the faith and foresight of those Old Chapel folk. Now the old place at the top of town had a struggle to keep the doors open.

I conducted worship there one Sunday; I found it a colossal great cold building where the small congregation looked lost among the vast pew area. The mighty organ seemed to drown the voices of the faithful little group who had gathered, and although they were a wonderful and saintly folk it was not easy for them to worship I thought. From the great pulpit I felt as if I ought to wait for a few hundred more people before I started the service.

I conducted worship there as often as I could, and befriended the people who were so faithfully supporting, but it was plain that the church's existence could not go on as things were. The buildings alone would have to have vast sums of money lavished upon it, and for what?

I could not see that there would ever be enough people attending for the income to meet even the running costs let alone the renovation.

I was asked to chair their meetings, and I could at least share what experience and help I could, but I was very careful not to suggest anything about closing the church. Who would ever want to buy such a decaying set of buildings, plus a fair sized graveyard attached, and in an area that was no longer the place where people wanted to live?

What I did suggest was that we should get together the two groups of Church Deacons for fellowship and support. This was readily agreed to by both churches and became a happy development. It was at one such joint meeting that the problem of the old Chapel came up, and I was surprised to hear one of the Old Chapel Deacons say that there was only one real solution. Either we must close this successful and busy town church here and all come and worship in the old Chapel building, or, close the old buildings and they must come and join forces with this one in the centre of town, and it was easy to see which of the two we should choose.

I expected some opposition to such a suggestion, for people are always loyal to their own place of worship, and everyone hates change, these old buildings at the top of town held such a wealth of sacred and happy memories; but everyone readily agreed now to this idea, and the meeting went on to discuss how such a merger might take place.

Over the following months the two churches often shared worship, and the idea became a proposal that the two churches should come together to form a new church in the premises of the popular town church, and having a new start it should have a new name. The only unsolved problem left to pray about was the Old Chapel Buildings and the graveyard at the top of the town.

Knowing that miracles take place when people pray, we prayed for a solution, God's solution! I don't think that any of us could see how it was possible for God to answer such a prayer, it seemed an impossible situation. Meanwhile we planned the great coming together with a special service. It was a great time for both churches and the amalgamation was completed with great joy, even though some from the old place were sad to cut with such happy past memories.

Reading the local newspaper I learned that the local Town Council were planning a new road-widening scheme at the top of town. This had no significance until I ran into one of the leaders of the local Pentecostal Church who told me that their church was right in the way of the proposed development, and that the Council had been trying to acquire their buildings along with other premises in the road.

It seemed that The Council had offered the Pentecostal Church alternative buildings, but nothing they offered seemed suitable, and there was a stalemate in negotiations. The Council had to re-house them but the church demanded something that they felt was suitable.

The Holy Spirit has His own way of doing things, and I found Him now giving me an idea.

The more I thought of it the more it appealed; finally I felt that I must try it. I knew the leaders of the Pentecostal Church and I phoned one of them and asked if he and the other leaders would meet me up at the Old Chapel building. A time was agreed and we met outside the Hall that was at the side of the old Chapel building.

It was a hall of reasonable size, of a younger date to the church, and well preserved. I explained to the Leaders that I wondered if it would make a good Pentecostal Church. I listed their objections as they looked around it, and out of the list I said that I thought I could have a new heating system installed, one or two other small items done just as they wanted, and the whole place redecorated to their own wishes.

At once they were keen on having the place as their new church, but what would it cost them? Boldly I suggested that if they left it to me it would probably cost them nothing. They went away excited, but agreed not to say anything to anyone until they were made a written offer, which they could then take to their members.

I had only met the Town Clerk a few times, and then rather formally, but I now made an appointment to see him in his office. I told him that this was a strictly informal meeting, but that I had an idea which might help solve some of his problems. We talked of his problem of re-housing The Pentecostal Church so that the road scheme could go ahead, and said that if the Council would make an offer for the whole site of the old chapel, (burial ground as well) The Pentecostal Church would, I thought accept, and move into the hall, if certain conditions were met, and I told him exactly what they would want.

My scheme pleased him, and he shared with me another problem, that the burial ground was also part of the road widening plan and that he was just about to write to the church over the proposed removal of some of the bodies there, and was not looking forward to the church's reaction.

The upshot of all this finally resulted in The Council buying the whole Old Chapel site, and receiving permission to remove some of the bodies in the burial ground under special conditions, to a special site in the cemetery, With the re-housing of the Pentecostal Church, and the proceeding with their road widening scheme. Everyone seemed happy, and the church was relieved of a possible burden that could have dragged on for years.

The way I see it, we had a problem, we took it to The Lord, and He answered it so perfectly that we could not have imagined such a perfect answer.

He also solved the problems of quite a few other people at the same time.

Yes, I would call it a miracle. I cannot see how it could have happened other than God working in the minds of everyone concerned, to the general good of everyone.

The two congregations quickly became as one, and now after all these years, the church still flourishes and is a real blessing to the whole community.

Chapter 18
MIRACLES WE FAIL TO NOTICE

As the years go by we are discovering more and more of the little wonders God has tucked into His world. At the time of their discovery they are regarded as "marvellous" but as we get used to them we take them for granted.

I read sometime ago that when Faraday was lecturing and demonstrating the new-found electricity, several newspapers of the day said "Electricity is all very marvellous but in practical terms What Good Is It?" Now of course our world is just about run by it and we take it all for granted. The same could be said for most of the world's discoveries and inventions.

So, what of all the miracles of our modern life that we have now grown use to? Does a miracle cease to be a miracle because we have got used to experiencing it?

The wealthy people in their great castles and houses, once used to employ minstrels to come into their home to provide music while they sat and ate. Now, the poorest can have a full orchestra play at anytime at the touch of a hand-held button, and it all takes up no more room than a small book. Miracle? It would be a hundred years ago, but not thought of as being so today. Miracles are only acknowledged in the concept of our mind!

Following one Sunday conducting worship in my church someone said to me "That which you said this morning was just for me, it was really helpful, what a pity that others who are too ill or infirm to come could not share the message". This thought haunted me in the days that followed, and I wondered why we could not take some of our Sunday worship out to shut-in members.

There was the tape recorder with its small cassette, but with elderly or sick folk it might be easy for them to press the 'record' button instead of the 'play' button and they would erase the contents, and they would feel very unhappy about that.

Then I found the answer (or the one higher up did) a cassette PLAYER, a machine that would only play, and not record. I purchased a small white little 'cassette player' and I took my own Cassette Recorder into the pulpit on Sundays, duly recording a selected part of the worship and the sermon.

Two of the congregation, a father and son, who thought it a good idea volunteered to take the player around to elderly members who could no longer get to church, and so a new ministry started. It proved to be highly successful, and was soon in great demand. Just imagine what elderly people, who had not been able to get to their church for several years, felt, when they sat and listened to what the whole church had enjoyed last Sunday. To them it seemed a Miracle.

Perhaps it would have been a miracle that was now forgotten but for an old scrapbook of press cuttings I still keep. The local newspaper had heard of this new ministry and had visited a home where the tape player was being used, and they had photographed the two volunteers holding the player beside two old ladies who had not been able to hear their own church service for years. As I look at that faded cutting today God seems to say "Remember what I did in answer to your prayers?" It gave happiness, made people feel that they were still remembered, and brought the Gospel to bear on their needs.

I sometimes wonder if there are some little miracles that never get off the ground because people cannot be bothered to encourage them. I think of the countless old people's homes where numbers of the elderly end up toward the close of their life.

There comes a time when those of advanced years cannot cope by themselves, and the only answer seems to be for them to go into a residential home for the elderly. All through my life I have visited these places, and I have encouraged the church to go in on a regular basis to talk to the residents and perhaps once a month take a little service. Just a few well-known Hymns, a Prayer, Reading, and story or talk.

It gives them something to think about, something that is different happening. Most of the time it becomes a routine of getting up, having meals, and sitting in a chair sleeping, with the television chattering away in the background with no one taking any notice.

Some have relatives who visit more or less on a regular basis, and what a special time that is for them... unless they get to the state where they can't recognise even loved ones. But there are quite a number of residents who never get a visit. Not all old people have children, and many have families who have moved to far away places or out of the country. No one visits these needy elderly. The friends they once had are too old themselves to go and visit, and they just have to sit with their memories of past days, and doze their last years away.

I once started a scheme to encourage people to visit such lonely old folk. I asked for people to pledge to visit and befriend one person on a regular basis. At first I had several who pledged to do so and they started to go to a particular person once a week, or once a month, as suited them. It worked quite well for a short time, and then there were months when they just did not get around to it.

They all had their excuses, but bit-by-bit the visiting stopped. It seemed easy to start such a scheme, people felt good in what they were doing, but there was no sticking to it, and the old folk wondered why their new found friends didn't come any more.

Lonely old people in homes feel that nobody cares about them anymore when no one comes to see them, and they are right, of course. Active people are just too busy to put themselves out to befriend them in our modern life. We just never make time. What could bring some lonely old soul something new to think about and that important feeling that somebody cares, that miracle of love; never happens. It's a little miracle that never gets off the ground!

The Funniest Miracle I can Remember

The interesting thing about being a Minister, is that you never know what is going to happen next. The phone constantly rings and you can never know who will be on the other end of the line or what they will want or say. The doorbell rings, and you cannot help wondering who you will find standing on your doorstep. It may be a tramp who will spin you a yarn with the hope of getting you to part with your money. Usually they want it for drink or drugs, and often you can smell drink on their breath even while they are talking.

Sometimes their stories are quite ingenious, most of the time you have heard their story before and it comes out almost like the well-rehearsed lie it is. Their father is dying in far away Scotland and they want desperately to get to his bedside before he dies. They want the fare, they will pay you back, please help them to get there. Usually I did not have that kind of money anyway so they had to be "sent empty away".

Very often the doorstep would reveal a genuine need, and you could do what little you could. Or it would be some mundane issue. Like the day when I answered the door to Mrs P. She was one of my Church Members and a loyal and kindly worker within the Christian Church.

Even as she stood there I could see that something was wrong. Her face was creased with pain, and her whole body was bent and stiff. "Come in" I invited "Whatever is wrong?"

She entered my study and slowly and very painfully sat in my armchair. "I've come about the Bible Society" she said. Recently she had been kind enough to take over as the secretary of the local branch of The Bible Society, and the job was new to her. She had come to discuss what to do.

"But you don't look well" I interposed "Are you in pain?"

"Yes, I'm in agony, I just don't know what to do with myself" she breathed, and the agony showed in her face and in every movement. "Two or three years ago I slipped on the ice one wintry morning and I fell and hurt my back" she moaned "It comes and goes, most of the time I get no pain at all; Sometimes it really hurts, but I can live with that; But sometimes, like this morning it is so bad I just don't know how to bear it." Tears ran down her face.

"Have you been to the doctor?" I asked.

"Oh he's seen me again and again, I've been to the hospital too, and had all sorts of treatment, but nothing changes it. It is so bad this morning... I suppose I ought not to have come out, but I thought I ought to try to carry on as normal, and it might just go."

I asked her "Have you tried alternative medicine?"

The pain made her pause before answering "Yes, it seemed to work at first but it didn't last long."

"Have you asked for prayer and the 'laying on of hands?'"

She paused, "No I haven't! I've prayed of course." She paused, "Somehow I never thought of that. As a Christian I should have thought of that shouldn't I? Would you do that for me now and minister healing to me?" she said tearfully. I told her that I would.

We sat quietly for a few moments and I prayed for The Holy Spirit to come and work through us for Mrs P's healing. I waited for a little longer and then did what I thought I was being led to do.

I walked over and stood behind the armchair. I prayed out loud, although I cannot now recall just what I said, I placed my hands upon her head. I called on the power of my Lord to heal her painful back, then I returned to my seat. I then asked her about her reason for coming and we discussed at some length the work of The Bible Society and the task she sought to do.

As we talked together I observed that she was no longer thinking of her pains, she smiled on one or two occasions and seemed to be more like her old self. I paused in our conversation to ask "How's your back? She stopped, and then she started to wriggle about in the chair. For such a heavily built lady I feared for the chair springs. Then she stood up, moved about, bending in different directions.

Then she did something I could never imagine her being able to do, this large lady bent down and touched her toes. What a sight! A more comical sight you just cannot imagine. I just could not help myself, I just had to laugh, she looked so funny! She then did a little gig about the room shouting "It's Gone! I'm Healed, What a Saviour, Praise God!... Look at me... No Pain at all".

After this it was not very easy to get back to discussions on the Bible Society, she was so ecstatically happy. She looked at me and said "Oh do let's say a prayer of thanks." So we did just that, and her Amens were loud and clear.

Whatever we discussed after that, the miracle she had experienced kept coming back into her conversation; I think that she will remember it for the rest of her life.

Now, I have known her not only for the ten years that I remained her Minister, but I have known her ever since: For years, at least once or twice a year she came to visit us in our retirement. Over these many years, and also in many phone conversations, I have asked her many times "How's your back?" she always says that she has never had a return of that back trouble. Once recently she said to me "Once The Lord fixes something like that, it never comes unstuck, and I shall be forever grateful, to The Lord Jesus and to you."

Chapter 19
IS THERE SUCH A THING AS A HOLY ATMOSPHERE?

I ask that question because so very many people seem to believe that there is such a thing as atmosphere, among people, in buildings, and found in certain places. I recall one of these TV Gardening programmes recently where some lady said that soon after she and her husband bought the house they both felt an atmosphere of peace and tranquillity both in the house but particularly in the garden. They did not know it when they purchased the house but later discovered that it had once been the site of an old monastery, which closed in the sixteenth century. We think that the Monks have left a Holy Atmosphere.

They laughingly said that they had never seen a ghost, but that the garden in particular was so peaceful that they often thought of the monks that might well have laboured in their garden, and somehow their quiet life of contemplation seemed to still give off an atmosphere of calm. Is that rubbish? Imagination? Or might they be right?

I have heard that the reverse is true, that a house or place that has witnessed murder or great unhappiness has an atmosphere reflecting what has gone on in the past. Are the tales told of The Tower of London true? Or are they made up for the visitors, or good advertising?

I frankly do not know the answer to this puzzling question, but I certainly believe that I do experience an atmosphere for either Godliness or Evil occasionally when I go into certain places.

Be that as it may, I do believe that some churches have an atmosphere, let me tell you what has influenced me.

A young lady attended my church one Sunday and naturally I made sure of talking to her after the service was over. She turned out to be a manageress for a large company of general stores and had been sent to the branch of that store in our town. She had arrived, and had been inspecting the store during one morning, and after lunch she decided to look at the opposition in the town. Right opposite our church was the Debenhams Store, she viewed it, and as she came out from her look around there, she saw our church standing at the top of the drive right opposite.

Crossing the road she walked up our drive, and entered the church. It is not a particularly beautiful building inside. Typical Free Church. No altar or pretty decoration, just a simple plain place of worship. She sat in one of the pews at the back, and told me that the atmosphere just got to her. She felt a deep peace, and a feeling of well being that convinced her that life was going to be good for her here in this town. She told me "I just did not want to get up and leave, there was a sense of God's presence, and the atmosphere of worship and inner joy."

She had started work on the following Monday but somehow all the week she looked forward to visiting that church which had attracted her so. Happily she found the act of worship to her satisfaction too and from that day on she became a regular part of the congregation. She found good friendship in a group of young people within our church, and they enjoyed walks and social activities which was ideal for her living on her own in a new and strange area.

She talked with me often, and came to make her profession of faith in Jesus Christ, and to join the church. It was a sad day indeed when she had to leave us a year or two later, but, she told me, the atmosphere of our church had introduced her to something that blessed her life and she was helped on her way through into the future as part of God's love became known direct through Christ and through fellow Christians.

What you will make of all this I do not know, but she considered it one of God's miracles.

The Man Who Had a Reluctant Miracle

I have never ceased to be amazed at Christianity and God's Church being so wonderful, so many people remain outside the joy and Blessing it brings for both now in this life and for eternity. You would think that people would be queuing up to be part of it. Thinking about this mystery I have to remind myself that The Devil works hard to keep people away, and "has blinded their eyes so that they cannot see". Also, people are so very ignorant of anything to do with the Spiritual side of life. And know little or nothing about God, or God's Church.

I have heard some weird ideas expressed about The Church. All of them untrue! That it is a moneymaking racket. When in fact it gives and gives sacrificially, and is the driving force behind most charities and help to all people. That it is 'Run By' a people or organisation at the top. When the truth is that for most of the churches, certainly all I have been associated with, The Church Members in the local Fellowship run and pay for everything, and are completely free of all outside control.

They sometimes say The Church is Old Fashioned! It is true that it changes slowly, and that many of the worshippers enjoy doing things in the way that they did when they were young. But not many people like changes anyway, whatever they believe.

The things of deep love and sincerity do change slowly. Like love for parents, pet animals, and things of sentimental value. But The Bible has seen more new translations in the last fifty years than ever before. We have kept some of the old hymns which people say they still love, but Oh the number of new hymns we have now! Prayer has changed in most churches, from an old language to a more up to date one. Yes we still have much of the old but we have the new too.

Here is an event that might make you think. The story of Peter Sims.

Peter was brought up in a very secular world. Only once was he ever taken to church. What kind of church it was I never asked him, but by his later conversation I think it was nothing like our church. When he came home from that visit he declared to himself and all who would listen "It was a load of rubbish, I didn't like it, and I shall never ever go to church again."

And that was where it stopped. The years went by and he kept to his word, and never went near a place of worship, not even for weddings and funerals it seems. His teens and twenties came and went, and I don't think he ever thought about God or Church.

At the end of his twenties he went to visit an uncle who lived far from his home.

There he was a bit shaken to discover that Uncle was a Christian and read his Bible daily.

Uncle never pushed his religion at Peter, but it came out in a most natural way in general conversation.

Hearing it in this way it came as a surprise to learn such things as were spoken about generally were to be found in the Bible. Words and quotations he thought of as worldly were from Scripture, and Uncle was always explaining such things to him.

He came to have a real affection for this Uncle, and this first visit became the start of several visits. His Uncle was constantly advising him to read the Bible for himself, but on the one occasion that he did try to do so he found that he did not know where to start and could not understand what he read. So The Bible was almost put in the slot with the church. Something he would not bother about.

Peter also had an Aunt who lived near him, and he often visited her, he now also discovered that she read her Bible and she also, like the far away Uncle, went to church. The Aunt was a member of my church, and she added to the plea for Peter to read the Bible, She also invited him to come with her to CHURCH.

One day the conversation must have got a bit confused, for when the Aunt asked Peter if he were free on Sunday morning, he thought it was to take her somewhere, and he agreed that he was quite free. "I have nobody to go to church with, Peter, it is so kind of you to say you will come with me." He was trapped!

Later he reasoned that he had only been to church once in his life, so it would not hurt to go just this once more. He knew that he would hate it, but it was only an hour or so, and it would please the Aunt. It would also confirm his decision that religion was a load of rubbish. He would certainly never go again he told himself. He went through the week dreading the visit to church, and priding himself that it would be the very last visit in his life.

So Sunday came. I entered the pulpit that Sunday quite unaware that the young man sitting next to one of my members was in a foul mood, but his face certainly showed it, he looked very unhappy. However, halfway through the service I noticed that his face started to change. He looked interested, and through the sermon he did smile at something amusing that I said, and I thought I had his attention.

As soon as the service was over I made my way to welcome him, and then to the back of the church to say "Goodbye" to those leaving. I don't remember him saying anything at the door, but it was nice to see him sitting with his Aunt, and I told him so. I did not suspect that it was something of a miracle that he came again next Sunday.

On his third visit I stopped him on his way out and started a conversation with him. Suddenly in the midst of the talk about his work, he broke off and said "Two Sundays ago I came just to please my Aunt, three weeks ago I had only been to church once before in my life. I hated it and vowed never to enter a church again, but coming here seems to have changed all this, This Church and everything is very strange and all new to me, I think I'd like to have a chat with you about it sometime."

Of course I had that chat. He told me that during that first visit to our church he had felt his anger over church just melt away. What I had been led to say during the service was "just for him". Was there really a God? Was it God talking to him?

Did God ever bother about ordinary people? What was he to do about God?

It was the start of many talks we had together, and slowly he came to realise that God and Church were not what he had thought, to know that God loved him and was available at all times to guide and help. That the church was just a group of ordinary believers who gathered to worship God and help each other on their Christian road.

This all lead to him attending our Bible Study group, and I must say that he enlivened the Bible study group no end. He was a person who called a spade a spade. His conversation was always down to earth. On one occasion I recall he made the comment about some passage "If God had said that to me mate; I'd have told Him to get on His bike!" It was refreshing to the group and a delight to me as I saw him unfolding toward God like a flower turning to the sun.

Peter made his profession of Faith in His Jesus in due time, and became a member of the church. He was part of the fellowship and family and we enjoyed him for a few years. Then sadly I was asked to pray through what he felt sure was God's will for him. It turned out to be so, and Peter Sims gave up his work, gathered his things together and left for Australia. I hoped that he would write to me so that I could follow up the friendship, but sadly, I have never heard from him since and I have never had his address.

Chapter 20

WHO KNOW GOD'S WILL?

When a Minister comes to a church there are usually one or two people on the roll of membership that are living far away. I was always a bit suspicious of such people because experience has taught me that some folk join the church and then move away to far off areas and we never see them again. But they seem to like to leave their names on the roll of members, when they should be transferring their membership to another church in their new area and getting involved with a new fellowship.

When I pointed to the name of Katherine Peel I met with a reaction of warm love and a firm rejection of any idea that she should be considered as no longer a church member. Our Katherine is just wonderful, and she will be back among us one day, you'll see!

It was therefore with great interest and keenness to meet her that I learned that she would be coming home on leave. It was then that I also learned that she had been living and teaching in the Middle East.

Soon after this I entered the pulpit to see a lovely young woman sitting in the side pew and I instantly knew that this was Katherine Peel. Our relationship in those early days was quite different each to the other. To me she was like one of my daughters, and I had a real love for her as such. Katherine however felt quite differently about me. She seemed suspicious of my preaching and my theology. And I think, of me.

I must say that I remember that The Holy Spirit was pushing me, rather than leading me, to make contact with her, and slowly we got to know and trust each other and discuss her problems.

Her mother, a widow, was naturally very concerned because the area abroad where Katherine was teaching was a war torn place, constantly in the news with reports of shellfire and bombing.

Katherine felt that The Lord was looking after her and the school, and there was no one else to do the work she was doing. The Lord had called her to do this work and was blessing her with good results in the school and much love and trust among the pupils.

Her time at home was over all too quickly and she returned to the danger area. We both promised each other that we would pray over the situation and seek God's guidance .We also agreed to let the other know of any answer that we felt was from God.

I prayed constantly for the guidance, and kept in touch with letters. As time went on I became more and more convinced that she would soon return and that all would be well. I then was given the answer to prayer that we had waited for. God told me clearly and surely that Katherine should return to the U.K. and that she would not be going back.

I wrote with the news I had received, and I expected her to write back that she had received the same message from God and would be coming home. To my surprise she wrote that she had no such leading from The Lord and that she would not consider any move until she herself was told so by God.

The days went by and I was looking for every post expecting to have a letter from her saying that she also now knew and would be coming home. As the fighting in her area grew worse I began to wonder what was going on. I knew for sure that Katherine should not stay; she did not get the same message. It was a time of testing for both of us, but particularly for me; could I be wrong?

I wrote to her again, and found that when I read it over before sending I had put in closing "We look forward to seeing you home again, it won't be long now." I could not recall writing it, but I sent it anyway.

As I remember it (it is a long time ago) things came to a rapid climax in her part of the world. The fighting increased, the school was closed down and the children scattered, and she received her order to go home, and she arrived soon after.

We met to share her future plans, and she had one big problem. She was a qualified teacher, but she was not qualified to teach in this country. The British authorities would not accept her as a teacher unless she went off to teacher training college and passed the British examinations.

Katherine was happy to have some time at home getting used to the change back to U.K. life, and getting over the tough experiences she had endured, but any direction from The Lord seemed to be missing as to what He required of her next. Once more I seemed to get the answer first, Why? I do not know. I knew that The Lord wanted her to obtain the English qualifications and go to College to get them.

Once more Katherine said, quite rightly "No, not until I get the message myself". And a little time passed before this happened, but when it did, it came at just the right time to start the course, and to find that there was a vacancy for her.

I have no idea just how difficult or easy it was for her, but she gained her English qualifications just as The Lord wanted her to, and as I can see now all these years later, it all happened perfectly timed and as the right thing to do. As always, God knows what He is doing and He does it wonderfully!

As Katherine settled down in my church, she became a great blessing to us all, she later fell in love with a young man named David, and I had the happy task of guiding them toward marriage. My eldest daughter became a bridesmaid, and I have a small photograph in my study today of that happy wedding day and view it with very happy memories.

From time to time through the years though I have wondered just what we were supposed to learn from the event. She was the one involved and in need of leading yet I seemed to know before she did what The Lord wanted her to do. To me, it does not seem to make sense. But the fact remains that the miracle of God communicating His will to his people is still there and in daily use by millions of Christians. What would we do without Him?

Katherine and her husband have kept in touch with my wife and I all down the years, with a Christmas card and a page of news about each other once a year. They joined the local parish church near where they live; they are a tower of strength to that church. Their children have grown up to trust The Lord, and both Katherine and her husband enjoy a career in teaching. Many times when I go to conduct worship at other churches I hear that Katherine was conducting their worship the previous Sunday, or is due to do so the week following my visit, somehow never seem to meet up to exchange pleasantries.

As I review this book before it is published I have been saddened to learn of her ill health and hospitalisation, and now she has just been called home to her Lord. I feel deeply for her family, but I rejoice in the fact that she loved her Lord and is safe in His love and care now and will be forevermore.

Chapter 21

BEING CALLED BEYOND YOUR TALENTS

In most of the churches I have been call to serve I have been blessed by having a Choir. Not only does a choir help everyone to enjoy a good sing, but, an Introit to start a service can helpfully get everybody in the right mood to worship God. The Anthem can also be a blessing in directing people's thoughts and can also help as a transition between one phase of worship and another.

There is no doubt that a good organist and choirmaster with dedicated singers can enrich an act of worship, but I found out once that a problem choirmaster can be a problem indeed!

The sad thing is that we all get older and sometimes when we do we lose some of our capacity to do what we have done so well in the past. If we can see that we are not doing something as well as we used to do and have the courage to admit it and stop, that is a good thing, but if everyone else can see that we are past it, except the person concerned... therein lies a problem.

Mr Miles had been a good, talented and loyal choirmaster for more years than most cared to remember. Some of his efforts in conducting the choir in great musical works had been beyond doubt memorable events, which many still recalled with pleasure. His capacity to get the best out of the choir was unquestionable; he was indeed a Master of The Choir. He enjoyed his work for The Lord and everyone else enjoyed the results of his talents.

Then Mr Miles grew old. With his advancing years came deafness, not much at first, but getting worse as he got even older. His spirit never faltered, he thought he was as good as he ever had been and therein lay the problem. Choir practice became an embarrassment to organist and choir.

Added to his deafness came some confusion, he talked of a B Flat that was not there, he said that they were off key when they were not, he asked for a note from the organist, did not hear it, and got cross when he thought he had not got the note and shouted for it long after it had been given.

The members of the Choir came to me to deal with their problem. They did not agree just how it was to be dealt with. One or two were horrified that he should be dismissed from his great, long and honourable service; they remembered the old days and respected him. Some said bluntly, "If he does not go soon, there will be no Choir or Organist, and there are limits to what we can put up with". I felt like the 'Pig In The Middle' and saddled with a job I would rather not tackle.

I slipped into a back pew during choir practice to see for myself how bad the situation was, there was no doubt that Mr Miles was no longer able to help the Choir sing well, there was certainly evidence that everyone got impatient with his obvious failures as a Choir Master, I would have to do something about it. As I felt right out of my depth I started with a great deal of prayer. I just did not know what to do about the situation.

Just as I was planning to visit him and talk to him about it, circumstances changed. Mr Miles caught Bronchitis and sent apologies that he would be unable to come. I now visited him in the roll of 'sick visitor' and was able to suggest that he take care because of his great age. I even suggested that he had been doing far too much and ought to think of retiring from his years of good service to God and his church, "We all have to stop sometime" I told him "you cannot go on until you are a hundred, And we must stop overworking you".

I thought that my efforts to sow ideas were rather poor, so I kept up prayer in faith that God would find some way out. Mr Miles was plainly planning a return to duties as soon as he felt better.

One of the Choir members managed to take the Choir Practice for the first week of Mr Miles' absence, and it just happened that I managed to get someone who was visiting in the district, and who was an organist of her church back home, to take the second week.

"I hear that you've got a woman taking my place" said Mr Miles when I visited him "Yes" I replied without going into details. "Mr Miles, I know that you are getting better, and everyone is so pleased. You must know that you are very well loved by everybody at the church, and we all know how wonderfully well you have served us over so many years, But I really do think, that with your problem of hearing, your advancing years, and you are not as strong as you used to be, you ought to seriously consider retiring as our Choir Master."

"Your health may improve, but your deafness and your strength are not going to improve, are they? It won't be easy for you to admit to yourself that you are not as good as you were in those great days of the past; but you will have to lay down that baton soon, why not now, while everyone is in happy remembrance of all that you have done, rather than see you grow less and less able to keep up your great high standard."

Tears welled up in his eyes, "I'll tell you something, you must not tell any of the others; they haven't noticed yet, but I have not done the job so well lately. You are right that I can't always hear, I used to have wonderful hearing. I remember...." He went off on some well-remembered story.

Three days later came a letter from him. "This will come as a great shock to you" he wrote "I am resigning from the post of Choir Master after... years". The letter was very gracious yet proud. We made a great event of his leaving the post; it even got into the local paper with his picture. The church and the Choir were pleased that the situation was brought to a happy conclusion.

The solving of one problem sometimes brings yet another problem to solve. Who would take Mr Miles' place? The visiting lady had returned from her visit to us, and there was just nobody to take over. Oh how I wish that people who tackle tasks would introduce assistants who could train to share the load and take over when needed. It rarely happens, sad to say.

I attended the next Choir Practice and talked to the choir, urging them to look out for a Choir Master, permanent or temporary. In the mean time I suggested music that they had done often before, and at the suggestion of one of the members I took over the task of conducting for the evening, it would be just a case of bringing them in to start together and keeping them going the way planned, or so I thought!

It so happened that during that week I discovered a booklet of choir pieces that were new to me, I photo copied these and distributed them among the choir. To my great relief they liked them and it was decided to do one each week as Anthems. The organist was extremely helpful to me and I found myself conducting the Choir for practice and on Sundays. I found that I rather liked the task, and even with my limited musical knowledge I seemed to do better than I thought, and had the support of the choir.

As Christmas came near I managed to get printed copies of some carols that I had on tape recordings with my favourite Choir. Having got permission to do these, we went into rehearsal. I knew just how they were sung from my recordings so I was able to get the choir to sing it just right. I was fast becoming a Choirmaster in the eyes of the church. They were hearing Anthems they had never heard before and now Christmas Music sung wonderfully well. I was pleased, the Choir seemed pleased and the church were well satisfied.

I now state quite definitely that I did not, and do not consider myself a Choirmaster. But I do believe that given the circumstances and need; God enabled me not only to fill the gap for several months but also to do it with the general happy approval of everyone. Can God lend you talents for a little while so that you can achieve something for Him? If this so, I can tell you this was a Miracle! In this story you may have noticed how many times things just seemed to happen right, to me there was a greater hand ruling the events, it certainly was not me.

It was an event in my life that although I enjoyed it I was very happy to bring to an end when we got a real Choirmaster to take over, for two young men, who were twins, joined the church, both were well qualified musicians, and from then onward the music side of the church just went from strength to strength.

Chapter 22

GOD CAN USE YOUR HOBBY

During the 1960's I had settled on making my Hobby the construction and running of a Model Railway, and for this purpose I later purchased a large shed measuring 10'x 9' so that I could house my Railway where it would be out of every ones way, and a place where I could go when I needed a break from work. This Railway Room was moved around with me whenever I changed my address. At the suggestion of the famous Rev: Wilbert Awdry (of Thomas The Tank Engine fame) I invented my own Island, The Island of St Francis, and each time I moved house I modelled a different part of the Island.

Whenever I managed to get some time off work I would journey to the bottom of the garden and lose myself in my modelling. I had power laid on for light, heat and for running power tools etc, also an Intercom system so that I could hear whatever went on in the house, and answer the front door and the phone, if I could run fast enough before the caller rang off!

As the years rolled on I suppose I became something of an expert on Model Railways, as I didn't have much money, I made items rather than buying them, and I was happy to pass on what ideas or help I had learned to the many who also were interested. The Hobby of Model Railways has a vast following all over the world; it supports a big industry from large manufacturers to small firms. There are also several Model Railway Magazines, one of which I was able to contribute to with articles, and answer questions, in my latter days of modelling.

One of the occasional enjoyments was attending Model Railway Exhibitions. Apart from the big Exhibitions held in most of the main cities and towns there are also small local exhibitions where modellers from a local area can run their layouts and show their skills for the public.

There has always been a fairly large Exhibition held each year in Bristol, and I always managed to visit this one, enjoying a day seeing what others had achieved and visiting the stands which sold almost everything you might need for the Hobby.

Visiting one of the stands one year I was tempted to buy a locomotive for my own layout at home. It was second-hand and at a bargain price. The only snag was that when I went to pay for it I discovered that I did not have enough cash on me. I told the stall holder that I would leave my calling card with my name and address, and go to the car park where I had left my cheque book, and return to pay for it within a few minutes. To which he happily agreed.

Soon after I left, a young teenager came to the stall and in buying something he asked if there was anyone who could help him with some problems he had with his model layout. The stallholder said that there was Reverend Gossage who might help, and he gave the lad my telephone number copied from my card suggesting that he phone me, I might help.

While writing out my cheque shortly after I was told about the young man's visit and that seemed the end of the matter. However, Later on that day I was contacted by this young man, Ted Pearce. He phoned to ask if I could help him. So I visited his home and dealt with the mistakes he had made on his model railway.

To say that Ted was a Railway enthusiast would be putting it mildly. His parents were not well off, and they lived in a Council House, but being their only child Ted was given everything they could afford, so Ted's room and much of the house was adorned with railway memorabilia. At some time or other Ted had tried painting, and some of the walls were decorated with Ted's paintings of trains. There were books on railways and every other kind of item that one could imagine that had a railway connection. Ted seemed to be a compulsive purchaser of anything 'Railway'.

Having met Ted he would now come round to my house; first he would phone up and ask if he could come to see me, and if I could be free, we would spend quite a bit of time together. Always the conversation was of railways, mainly of The Great Western Railway, and when he was not attending the college just near my house he was visiting some preserved line and coming back to show me his latest memorabilia and talk about his trip.

We never talked about anything other than railways, although he must have been aware that I was a busy working Minister, but one day he suddenly just arrived on my doorstep asking if he could talk to me as he was in trouble.

I took him to my study and there he told me that he had just been thrown out of College, It appeared that he had lost his temper with another student, started a fight, and ended up by throwing chairs. He had been so violent that he had to be restrained and put outside the college premises with the statement that he was banned from the College, and that if he were seen there again they would send for the police.

I spent quite sometime with Ted that afternoon, and finally we got to the position where he promised faithfully that he would never loose his temper like this again, and that if I could get him back into the College he would apologise to all concerned and settle down to work hard never offending again.

The next day I contacted the head of the College, and I started to persuade him to take Ted back. It was not an easy task, but finally they agreed to see Ted by appointment and to talk to him. I briefed him on his behaviour at such a meeting, and, dressed in his best, he duly humbled himself, apologised to all concerned, and gave his assurance that such a thing would never occur again.

From that day onward Ted not only soaked me with his endless railway conversation but also shared with me all his problems over his behaviour to his Parents, College, and the things he felt that he was doing wrong. He had lived a rather sheltered life, did not get on with other people, especially those of his own age, and often felt that the world owed him something. Then there were times when he felt himself a useless nothing, and other times when he wanted to throw his weight about and boss everyone about. I think that I was the only one that he did not want to fight, and I was his only friend.

This all went on for some time, and I gave Ted as much time as I could, always trying to improve his thinking and attitudes. Then came the day I shall always remember.

And this story is honestly told just as it happened.

I was working in my study when quite suddenly God spoke to me! Let me make this clear, I did not hear a voice, but my mind was filled suddenly with my Heavenly Father's presence, and He spoke through my mind, but they were not MY thoughts. I just knew My Lord was there and speaking, His words were clear and commanding. And Quite unmistakable.

"Take a piece of paper and write this down" the voice said. As I placed the paper on my desk I wondered whatever was happening. The voice continued when I was all ready "Write- Ted is going to Phone" I wrote it down. "Ted wants to come and see you now". I wrote it. "Ted does not want to talk about trains". I wrote it. "Ted wants to talk about God". I looked at what I had written "Now put it away where Ted cannot see it, and leave it there" I slipped it just under the Blotting Pad on the desk. I waited, but nothing more came, nothing else happened.

I reasoned, I had not been thinking about Ted, I had been busy with something else. Did this really happen? I had another look at what I had written then slipped it back under the Blotter. "Strange" I thought, and I started to get back to my work. Then the phone rang. It was Ted, could he come round? "Yes" I said and he put the phone down. It was unlike Ted, for he usually had a conversation or told me what he was coming for.

Ted arrived and came into my study in silence. We sat in two armchairs and I waited. Ted seemed a little 'up tight' and was obviously doing some powerful thinking, and then he said "I don't know what to say". "Ted" I said "Do me a favour and go to my desk, look under my Blotter on my desk, you'll find a piece of paper there, just read it". Ted got up and walked over to the desk, took out the paper and he stood and read it, he read it more than once I think, then he turned to me. "How did you know that" his mouth was open in amazement. "That is what The God you want to know about can do" I told him, "I wrote that at His command just before you phoned". It was the perfect opening to a discussion about God,

He read it out loud "Ted is going to phone, Ted wants to come and see you now, Ted does not want to talk about trains, Ted wants to talk about God.... How did you know? How did HE know? Is He Real? I've come to you because you are different from anyone else I know, you KNOW God don't you!"

"Yes" I told him "I know Him and walk with Him all the time."

We spent a long time together, Audrey came and served tea and cakes, and we still talked on.

I told Ted that he would never be able to deal with his problems by himself, none of us ever can, What he needed was His Heavenly Father, I told him how Jesus loved him and gave His life for him. Finally I prayed with him and then he prayed. He sat there telling God about his failures, and how sorry he was, finally he asked Jesus to come into his life and run it completely, to make him what ever God wanted him to be.

The radiance on Ted's face when his prayer was over was wonderful to see; I had seen it before in others in similar circumstances. In a sense some of that radiance seemed to stay there with him always, he now even looked different. God had called him and Ted had responded, all was now well with Ted, his life from now on was to show it.

Ted now started coming to my church, I introduced him to a group of wonderful young people at the church who were going around together, and Ted was accepted as one of them. He had a fresh approach to his new faith, which seemed to be attractive to others and he was now gentle but outspoken about his faith. The new Ted was so different from the one I had known before. He was just a new creature. A delightful change!

Everybody seemed to be attracted to him, he was friendly, outgoing, and now enjoyed talking to anyone. His obsession about railways dissolved into a slot that was no longer more than an enjoyable hobby, and any trace of temper and moods seemed to have vanished altogether.

For three years Ted enjoyed being with our church family, He went through some tough times, his Father died, and I was able to help him through this, as well as taking the funeral. Later his Mother died also and he was to be left without a home, as the Council would not allow him to take over the tenancy of the Council House he had always known as home. He had to go through the heartbreaking process of leaving his home and finding some accommodation, life was not easy for Ted, but with the power of his new Lord, he came out on top.

But there were many very happy times too, especially I recall his twenty-first birthday which was celebrated in our home with all the young people making sure he had a great time. And nearly ducking him in our fishpond! Ted was just fun to be with.

Then Ted fell in love. She was a member of the local Baptist Church, and not surprisingly he left our church to join the Baptist Church. There he was also made very welcome although I lost much of the detail of his life. With the kindness of some Baptist friends we kept in touch. Ted lived in a caravan, and courted the young lady. I did not see so much of him.

Then one Sunday morning he attended his Baptist Church as usual. Some members had invited him back for lunch, but he said that he would go back to the caravan and change first, for he always dressed nicely to attend church worship, but preferred his ordinary dress afterwards.

The time for the lunch ran on and Ted did not arrive, finally one of the sons of the house went to the caravan to see where he had got to. Ted had had some kind of fit, collapsed, and died.

It was a shock to everyone. But I believe that all the trumpets sounded for him on the other side. I look forward to seeing him again, and one of the first things I think I shall say to him is "Have they got any trains up here Ted? What about the G.W.R.? God's Wonderful Railway?"

Chapter 23

GOD ANSWERS A CRY FOR HELP!

Of course every church has its problems, and its problem people. Some churches are keen, enthusiastic and just great to minister to. Other churches seem to cause a Minister great unhappiness.

I recall feeling very despondent for quite a long period in one church. Some of those I had to work with were constantly in opposition to all that I did, and no matter what I tried, nothing seemed to go right. Of course we all get times like this, but when the period goes on and on, life can be very unhappy.

The Congregational Federation contacted me at that time, to say that I had been nominated to be National President of The Federation, which was a very great honour indeed. I prayed about it and felt that I would be able to tackle such a big task, and left it in the hands of The Lord as to whether I might be voted into such a position. Of course I wanted to share this news with my church, so I took the matter to a special Deacons Meeting after the Sunday Service, telling them of the honour I had received.

Led by one most outspoken office bearer, the Deacons took the view that I could not be spared for the time I would have to take away from my church duties and they were against my letting my name go forward. So I wrote sadly to decline the honour, writing to say that I could not stand. It was just one more disappointment and feeling that my people did not care.

Of course we all have our 'off days' and I remember that I certainly got one on a certain Monday during that bad patch. It was one of those days when everything seems to go wrong. As one lady told me the other day when she was going through such a day. "I told myself, if one more thing goes wrong I'm going to go to bed until this day is over". I knew just what she meant! On this Monday just everything seemed wrong. People that I visited were out; two patients in hospital were unavailable to see as they were having treatment. And so the frustration built up.

I finally called in to see one woman who I hardly knew, but I had heard that she had been in hospital and I thought she would appreciate a visit from me, but here I had to endure an hour of her unhappy complaints about her treatment, her lack of friends visiting her and all her pains and troubles caused by her treatment. Her incessant voice of moans and grumbles, and the "I said to him, and he said to me" unwanted information that I had to sit and listen to was too much for me. I reached my car at last deeply depressed, and just sat, and I could have wept. "Take me away from this church and district". I cried out to The Lord "I have had enough".

I did not realise it, but God had heard my cry. The next morning I had a phone call from a church some fifty miles away. They needed help and advice from someone who was an experienced Minister and from three sources they had been given my name. After a special Deacons Meeting and also a Church Meeting, the Church Secretary had been asked to contact me. Would I be able to give them a Sunday to conduct worship at their church so that I could discuss with them their church's needs. I felt that the least I could do was to help this unknown church with whatever problem it had. I also felt very strangely drawn to the whole situation.

Having told my own church Deacons about this cry for assistance, I arranged for someone to take my services and I journeyed to their church one Sunday, and as I arrived in very good time I was able to hear about their problem even before the morning service started.

They had had no Minister for three years because they simply could not afford one, they had hired their Manse (Minister's house) out on a temporary basis to help raise income, and had been saving money for the purpose of calling a Minister.

The church had now enough money to provide for a Minister for a period of three years, but after this there would be no money left unless the church income increased substantially. After much prayer many in the church felt that they should now call someone, and this had now come to a head because the tenant renting The Manse was leaving it, and that source of income would naturally stop and the house stand empty.

In the afternoon I met with the Deacons to discuss the issue and help them. I felt at once that this was a church that had great faith, and had been prepared to tackle the situation sensibly, and work hard for a solution.

After a time of prayer together I advised them to seek a Minister as soon as possible and to be honest with whoever they viewed saying that the ministry was for three years unless finances increased to make it possible to extend that term.

Quite suddenly the atmosphere in the meeting changed to one of happy expectation. Everyone present believed that this was the right way forward. Then the question just had to come up. Did I know of anyone seeking a change of Ministry? Try as I did I just could not think of anyone that I knew who might even remotely be likely to change at that time. Strangely I never even thought of my own situation.

It was only over tea that the Church Secretary asked "How are things going in your present church? I suppose you would not consider coming here to be our Minister, we would so benefit from someone like you". Although hearing it in words it came as a bit of a shock, I did at that moment feel strangely warm and happy at the idea. I explained that I, or any Minister, would welcome such a challenge, but that I was settled in my present church and had no indication that I was called to change. "Whatever happens it Must be from The Lord". I told her. That was the end of the matter as far as I was concerned. To go through a bad patch was no excuse for me to run away from the church God had called me to serve.

I heard nothing for just over a week, and then a letter came from the 'problem' church. I expected that it would be a thank-you letter for going to help them and for taking their services. It was not!

The Church had met to hear the Deacons report and had instructed the Secretary to write to me, not just to express their thanks, but to say that much prayer had been made for guidance and the whole church was convinced that I should be their next Minister, and that therefore they were now Offering me a unanimous Call to be their Minister.

It is strange, but even as I read the letter I had a strong feeling that I would be their next Minister, and that God was in this. In my mind I heard my own passionate cry "Take me away from this church and district, I've had enough!" As the days passed, I became convinced that my discontentment had been God's way of calling me away from this church and I saw quite vividly that God was calling me to leave the church I was now serving; that my unhappiness was due to my failure to see His will in the matter.

I gave it time, I phoned the new Church Secretary to discuss many matters, and I thought it all over and I prayed, Oh how I prayed! My Lord just smiled down at me waiting for me to agree that this was what He was wanting me to do. I really had a feeling that He was standing just slightly behind me and to my right, waiting for me to say what I believed to be true. The moment that I agreed to the change I felt waves of happiness roll over me, and I knew that I was doing the right thing.

"When we walk with The Lord in the light of His Word what a glory He sheds on our way".

There was only one thing that marred the happiness of the contemplated move, and that was that one of my daughters was going through a difficult patch in her life, and she just did not want to move away from her friends and settled life. I agonised over this for many hours, and made much prayer. The only answer I received was that what I was doing was The Lord's will in moving, that all was going to be in His hands, and this was where I just had to go ahead trusting that all would be well. It was not easy though!

If only we could see ahead how simple life would be. Looking back now I can see that it was the right decision, that all did work out well, for us as a family, for me and for the new church and ultimately for my daughter.

To my surprise my resignation to my old church was taken calmly, though with many people there was a genuine sorrow at my departure. They were to call one of our greatest Ministers, a woman of great leadership quality. I later learned that she visited the people who had been my main problem and told them straight that she would have none of their nonsense, and firmly put them in their place, a thing I could never have done. She won the hearts of the people and did a fantastic job, far better than I could have done, it was just what The Lord wanted.

She was, in turn, followed by a man that I had had some influence in bringing into the Ministry, and he also was well loved I think. The church is doing very well today under yet another fine Minister. God knew just what He was doing!

"I know who holds the future, and He guides me with His hand, with God things don't just happen, everything by God is planned". We sing it, but do we believe it?

As for my new church. Within six months the income of that church rose to the level that would ensure my future stay with the church more than the three years. In fact I was to stay ten years until I retired from the fulltime Ministry. A daughter was to go through a very tough period but would, during that ministry come to commit her life to God, she was later to be involved with a Christian Radio Ministry abroad, where she had her own evening programme to India, and nightly she would proclaim God's message to more people in one evening than her Dad had spoken to in his whole life.

Today she is happily married, and together they run their own Ministry of Christian Radio, Television and Video.

It was a very important period for all four of our children. One cannot help but be concerned over ones children's future, and just trusting in God always seems to be tempered with the strong feelings that WE have to do just the right things for them. Looking back now I can only be thankful to my Lord for the way HE handled each of them, for now, all four are married, and settled in life, we have seven grandchildren, and that the eldest daughter went to Canada to be Head of a small Christian School, The other is doing the dedicated work nursing in the Intensive Care Unit of our local hospital. Our son is a Senior Engineer in BBC Television and a keen Christian, with his family.

As one thinks of the care and concern experienced over their growing up one can only see these end results as one of God's precious Miracles, and be extremely thankful. It is never easy to be a parent, but easier if one's children are committed into the hands of God. I never stop talking to God about them, and He just smilingly cares for them.

I think that it is a great pity that we all tend to view each day as a repeat of yesterday, or just another day! If we look at life as it is, a daily adventure, always into the unknown, it may be a little frightening, but it does cut out boredom and make life a challenge. It is then that we need to look back into the past days and see the miracles that have happened, large or small, and gain faith to go forward knowing full well that He who created the universe and created me, knows what He is doing and planned it all before He started the whole thing: So all will be well!

Seeing that long ago I committed every thing I am and have to my Father in Heaven, I tend to start every day with the thought "I wonder what He will do with me today". Looking back I can see that the outcome of much of my daily living has resulted in miracles.

Every day we communicate to other people something of what we are, and what we think, it changes or challenges them. To influence someone else, can be tragic if it is a bad influence; but perhaps a miracle in another's life if it changes them for the good. and we all do influence others, all the time;

The Simple things that God does

Sunday by Sunday the preacher enters the pulpit, after much preparation, in order to lead the congregation to God's throne of all goodness. Praying that The Holy Spirit will use what is delivered. The service proceeds as planned, but at the end of all that is done there is no way of knowing what the result may have been to those who sat in the pews.

As the Minister shakes hands with the departing congregation he will receive various expressions of "thanks", but there are occasions when he gets a glimpse of what has really been received from his efforts.

I remember Mr R who in expressing sincere thanks for the sermon added one Sunday "I get an a great deal from your sermons, likc this morning". I asked "What in particular?" He paused for quite a long time, then said "Don't get me wrong, nor ever think that I am not getting a real blessing, but usually quite early in your sermon I get hit by some point you make, and I stop listening after that as I take that one point and think it through, and apply it to my own situation. I don't hear the rest of what you say, but I go home really helped and feeling good".

That was one person's way of getting Blessed. There are times when someone can hear what is preached but take it quite the wrong way. I recall a woman named Joan, she did not like me very much, I did not know if this feeling was true or my imagination,

She was certainly a bit cross with me when I came to her pew after one service. She greeted me with "Mr Gossage, We are not your family". I did not know what to say to that "How do you mean? What have I said?" I asked. "Calling us family, I am not Your Family, nor do I want to be". She crossly said. It is at this kind of point that either The Holy Spirit leads you to say just the right thing, or you think up the answer long after the conversation is over.

I looked her full in the face, "The first prayer that you and I said together this morning was 'Our Father'. You called Him **your** father, and I called Him **my** father, If He is Our Father, you and I must be Brother and Sister." I paused for a moment, then, "In any family where there are children, brothers and sisters may not get on very well together, but they cannot deny their joint parentage". Her anger disappeared. I smiled "As the children grow up together they often grow to like each other you know, I think Our Father wants us all to try to love each other". A smile broke from her face, she paused, and then said "I'm sorry, I misunderstood what you had said this morning. You are quite right, we must all try to love each other in God's Family".

I wonder just what you will make of this my next story. I had a wonderful woman in one of my churches, regular in attendance and loyal. Her husband never came to church nor seemed to have any religious faith. They had two daughters who came to church with their mother.

As the daughters grew into their teens I suspected that their interest in church going was not all that enthusiastic and I wondered what I could do about it. My prayers over this got the answer one day when I thought I might give them both something to do in the church. I asked one of them if she and her sister would like to help us out putting the hymn numbers up on the board. The morning could be done if they came just a little earlier, and the evening could be done after the morning service was over.

She turned me down flat. She was not going to come to my church any more, she would be going to a much more lively church elsewhere. I understand that she went with a friend to a local charismatic group, Unhappily she ruined her whole life ending up having an illegitimate child. Which, all credit to her, she has loved and cared for ever since.

The other daughter agreed to take on the task and faithfully did the hymn boards week by week, it kept her coming to church, and now she has grown into a lovely young woman. Although I understand, after I had left the church, she went to worship elsewhere. But she still keeps in touch with me and still goes to worship God every Sunday.

Yes these are simple things that God does, He respects each person's right to do things their way, but He is always there to help us to be better than we were .It is a miracle that He still works for our betterment when we leave Him out of our life most of the time.

Chapter 24

ENTERING A NEW PHASE OF MIRACLES

In my Ministry I have discovered that God sometimes changes ones talents or abilities.

I have always felt that I reached young people and children very well, in fact over the years I had come to think of myself as a man that was 'with it' as far as the young were concerned. Imagine my shock one day when chairing the meeting with Sunday School and Youth Leaders I found that the meeting was looking for someone else to reach their young, and not me.

It was only when I went home and prayerfully thought over the matter that I realised that now my own children were grown up I did not know just how young people thought and talked anymore.

Asking children what they had received for Christmas for example I did not know what the latest craze was, or the toys of the moment.

It was not that I could no longer communicate with children and young people, I could; but to know just what the 'in thing' was and the latest slang expression, I was lost.

The Lord has the kindest way of changing us, just before I came to the last church before retirement I was playing host to the local College Annual Service. It was the custom to hold it at each local church in turn, and it was now our turn. To them I was an unknown Minister for few went to church, or went to other places of worship.

When conducting such an act of worship there is always an atmosphere, and on this occasion the spirit of the meeting was just right. We had a wonderful service, and on several occasions there was a roar of laughter, which told me that they were with me and enjoying things.

My daughter was one of the students seated in the church and as soon as we got home together she was very enthusiastic. "Dad, you were wonderful, I was so proud of you, and it was great to hear everyone's comments after, you were really with it."

It was also a message from God as far as I was concerned when one of the lecturers phoned me to thank and praise me for the service, "which really reached them."

So I was shown that I could still reach the young, but I was certainly not one of them anymore, I had lost that gift.

The skills of reaching the young were not completely lost I discovered. It was at another Sunday School Teacher's meeting that I was faced with their great concern that the Teaching Guides which they followed each week were not being as helpful as they once had been. Much discussion took place but the final outcome was that I undertook to write a Teaching Guide, in which we covered the whole Bible twice during the period of a child's coming into and Sunday School and reaching Teen age.

The Lesson Guides that I wrote were for each age group and so arranged so that all the books of the Bible were covered and the main teaching and message was taken from each. It was a mammoth task, and based on two five-year sets of lessons. I think that I only produced the first three years or so before the teaching Staff voted to return to Scripture Union Lesson Guides, and my further labours were not needed. But somewhere in the attic today there still lies the remains of my efforts at producing Teaching Guides with the expression work to be used all laid ready. Foolish though it seems, I just cannot bring myself to throw all that work away, but someone will one day I expect.

However I was soon to learn that God may take away, but He also gives too. Now I was given a new healing ministry. Having moved to the last church before I would retire ten years later, I became aware of the new ministry when I went to visit one of names on my new church members list. They were a lovely couple with teenaged children.

I sat there in their little home chatting, and getting to know them. During the conversation I learned that both Vivian and George were deeply concerned that Vivian was yet to make another visit to the hospital the very next day. I asked them which hospital it was that she was to attend, It was a hospital that I had not heard of, and when I enquired about it, it turned out to be a hospital for the treatment of mental disorders, She had been attending this hospital for years, on and off and now and she needed to go back again for treatment.

Every so often Vivian did and said strange things, she did not seem to know what she was doing and her mind just went. She could not remember things and her behaviour could be dangerous. Especially dangerous in the kitchen they found.

I pointed out that Jesus had healed people far worse than she, and recalled stories of such healings from scripture. I cannot now recall just how the conversation went, I know we talked a bit about having Faith and trust in Jesus and that it ended by them asking me to pray for Vivian's healing. I placed my hands on her head and asked Our Lord Jesus to heal her. Following the prayer we agreed that Vivian must attend the appointment the next day as planned, and then the subject was dropped for the rest of the visit.

I was working in my study the next afternoon, when I had a phone call from Vivian. She said "I have just come home from the hospital. It's been a rather strange experience". She paused "They had a bed booked for me, but they said it was not ready just then and so the usual tests were to be done elsewhere. They did the tests in a small room and I waited for sometime before they informed me that there was something wrong with the tests they had just done, and that they would have to do them all again."

She sounded a little excited as she told me, "I began to have more faith that The Lord had healed me when they did the tests the second time, and they didn't look too happy. One of the doctors came out to the little waiting room where I was, and he explained that they thought there was a fault with the equipment, and he was sorry but the test would have to be done yet again, after they had checked up on their equipment."

"At long last they had me in to do the tests yet a third time, with several doctors now in on the act. In the end they just said that there seemed to be an improvement in my condition and that it would not now be necessary for me to come in at all. I was to go home and continue the tablets I had, and see my own doctor in about a week's time." The voice now came over in triumph "I'm Home, I feel great, and I know I am healed."

I had another phone call from George later, when he came home from work, and he had a rather questionable enthusiasm, "It sounds wonderful, do you think she really is cured, and will it last?" He asked.

I spent a little time with them in Thanksgiving, when I called on them later that evening.

The next few weeks proved that healing had taken place. Vivian no longer did the silly things she had been doing, her mind was clear, and she was 'like it was when I was a girl', to use her own expression. Her mood changed, and to use her husband's words "It's like having a new wife." To which Vivian replied "You better not let me catch you with a new wife! Unless it's me."

Although all this seems like an instant miracle, it was to take another year of slowly cutting down and finally leaving off altogether the medication she had been taking. They were working with the doctor and it was considered the wisest way forward. Today, all these years later, she is still fully normal and has never showed any sign of anything that indicated mental trouble. It taught this couple, and some of their friends that. There Is a God who heals. And He does it perfectly.

As I write this, it must be some twenty-six years ago that I first made that visit. I have been back to that church quite a few times and as soon as they see me that couple come rushing over to greet me with beaming faces and reassure me that Vivian is still completely cured, she has never has any sign of her old trouble, Thank God.

As for the doctors, as usual they said nothing, but perhaps they tried to reason such things out in some rational way.

Christian doctors are often seeing the hand of God at work in their daily lives, and they recognise it as such, giving God the Glory. Those not so fortunate to know Him have to find secular ways of accounting for the works of God. They acknowledge that there are many mysteries in life that are past finding out as far as they are concerned!

Chapter 25

THERE WERE THOSE THAT DID NOT SEEM TO GET HEALED

We have thought of those who have received real blessings and healing directly through the hand of God, through prayer, the 'laying on of hands', sheer Faith, and The anointing with oil. It is only right that we should say that countless people of all ages receive healing through the ministry of doctors, hospitals and nurses.

Over the years I have had conversations with quite a few doctors, and have always sought to discover their views on healing. I have yet to find a doctor who did not tell me that the patients' mental outlook (or Faith) had much to do with their healing. The following factors seem to be accepted. Where a person does not want to get well, or even does not want to live, there is a strong possibility that their mental attitude will affect the results of any treatment they get.

That where a person believes that they going to be made well, this too will affect their recovery. More than one doctor has told me that even if coloured water was prescribed to some people, and they believed that this was a good medicine that it would cure them and they would get better. The state of mind is powerful.

Against this is the fact that our creator has made the body to be self-healing, and under certain circumstances the body will get well anyway, all by itself.

Now I acknowledge that all this is generalisation and theory, but there seems to be no doubt that a person's mental attitudes are an important factor in most aspects of their life. The principle of 'The power of positive thinking' has a real and probably vital aspect in life happiness.

All this concludes that the knowledge of the doctor combined with God's desire and power to heal certainly is the normal way to healing. A doctor can bring broken bones together and hold them still, but it is God who has given the principle that does the healing and re-growing. It is the general principle that in life, God and man need to work together.

Just as a doctor has to face the fact that no matter how hard the trying, and how good the skill, some patients do not get healed, so this must be faced in what I would call the spiritual world. As illustration, I recall this story, which still haunts me of my failure.

I had a godly woman in my church who had great faith, and was living a good life of service to others and to God. Her husband was suddenly taken sick, and I went to visit him. At the request of both him and his wife I prayed for his good health to return, but nothing seemed to happen. I was asked to hold a brief service of 'laying on of hands', and as I did so I felt that God was telling me that the husband would get better.

There was some improvement in his condition, and I told the wife that I felt sure that he would soon be up and about. I was wrong! Within a few days he got worse and he died. It was a very great shock to everyone. I felt, and still feel that I let her down badly, I should never have told her that he would recover. It probably did not help the woman to deal with the situation, it caused a greater shock, which may have damaged the whole grieving process, and I felt that there was something of a barrier between us over all the succeeding years that I knew her. She herself died just a few years ago and I hope that she has now forgiven me for my mistake.

I have to admit that I do not know how the sharing with God of some situation in prayer, can bring about a healing. I cannot see how anyone laying their hands upon another can bring God's healing power, nor do I understand how anointing with a small drop of olive oil can make any difference to the health or sickness of anyone. Perhaps it shows God an act of Faith on our part. But not understanding things has never stopped me from using such means of Blessing.

As I type these things on my computer, I do not have any idea just how the computer can accept my thoughts and transfer them into a book, but such ignorance does not make me stop writing. No one really knows just what electricity is but we still switch on the light. And it works.

One thing I do recognise is that there is much sickness of body, mind and spirit in many people around me. I feel for the suffering of others and wish it could be relieved. Like any compassionate human being I would do anything I could to ease or remove what someone else suffers. My Bible tells me that there are things I can do, I can pray, and under certain circumstances, I can do other things like laying hands on a brother or sister in the Name Of Christ and that God will honour my obedience. I am not urged to learn how God uses such actions.

The thing that I have never discovered is whether there are set conditions, and if so what those conditions are for healing. There seems to be strict conditions to the working of many things. Going back to the illustration of electricity for example, there are strict conditions as to how it must be generated, conveyed to the place of use (cables) the way it must be handled and just how the resulting service is to be obtained. Does the same creator who thought that lot out, have set rules for the delivering of His healing power? Are we ever going to explore and find out?

The Life of Jesus Christ seems to show that His Ministry of healing was to God's People, Israel, The Jews. Yet He did heal a woman's daughter who was outside that faith, but He was very reluctant and had to be persuaded to do so. He did heal a centurion's servant but only after the pleas and reasoned persuasion by some of God's people. So is God's healing mainly for His own people? Does His healing only flow to those who are at one with Him, and does it depend on our oneness with Him. How does this tie up with Jesus' words "Your Faith has made you whole."

When we are given a gift, we have to accept it, receive it, unwrap it, and use it before we get the benefit from it. Maybe the same applies to the gifts of God.

Always in need of some leisure activity, I was persuaded by a Bowls enthusiast to join a Bowling Club on one occasion. The fact that I was no good at it, because my small hands were unable to hold the ball very well and that I later gave it up, has nothing to do with the story.

I did get to meet new people, and one man knowing that I had 'Reverend' in front of my name tackled me about Christian Healing. On discovering my views he almost got to his knees to urge me to visit his suffering wife.

She was willing for me to visit her, so I went to see her. She had been ill for sometime and although she was not a church goer she seemed to have a faith in God, and readily agreed to all I said concerning God's love for her and His desire to Bless her. I prayed for her healing, and I visited her regularly, even laying hands upon her for her recovery. Nothing seemed to happen! Week after week I was praying with her, talking to her, seeking to find out what might hold up the healing process, Nothing happened! As time went on I found the visits were more and more hard for me to bear, I prayed for guidance, but none came. In the end I had to give up and stop visiting.

The questions that I asked then, have never been answered. Why was I introduced to the situation in the first place if nothing was to come out of it? Why did no healing come, and why did God give me no guidance as to what He wanted me to do? Why did I feel guilty when I finally gave up trying?

This book has contained stories of some wonderful things that God has done, and if you have felt it all seemed easy, these thoughts that I share as my failures show that it has not always been 'A Bed Of Roses'; there have been thorns.

While the resulting Blessings that others have received through the Ministry God gave me have given me joy and deep satisfaction of Faith, there is the other side which I have to confess has at times brought sadness and plain exhaustion. I recall that Jesus once said that He knew a certain woman had been healed because power had gone out of Him. There were certainly times when I have felt weak and exhausted after Ministering Healing even though Healing Power was from God, not from me personally.

I am reminded that there was also a time when someone was brought to the Disciples and they could not bring healing. Their question to Jesus still comes back to me at times, they asked "Why could we not heal him? ". Did Jesus really say that Prayer and Fasting was needed, then heal the boy without those two factors?

To me Miracles are a fact, but why is it that some Healing Miracles don't last for a life time. To this question I think I have an answer through the following story.

I recall Mrs Greatly. She was a woman who was always unwell, constantly visiting the doctor, and had been in hospital several times. I would visit her, and spend an hour or more talking to her, and she would end up by being full of faith and ask for;

'The Laying on Of Hands' I would Minister to her and she would be fine, full of health, and praising God that she had been healed.

A few weeks later her husband would ask me to call again, and the whole process would take place again. She was ill and full of moaning over her lot. I would talk for another hour or more, I would Minister to her again and she would feel wonderful and thankful. This went on for two or three years, in fact she once said that my visits were like a bottle of medicine to her. (But one bottle should have been enough I thought)

Then came one visit which was something in the nature of an S.O.S.

Her son was getting married in only a few days time and she wanted above all else to attend and be fit for the wedding. As we sat there talking, I shot up a silent prayer for guidance. I got an answer at once, I knew what to say.

After I had talked for another half an hour I made a solemn promise to her from God that if she believed and never doubted, and repeated certain Bible texts that I would give her every day, she would not only attend the wedding but feel well all through the day.

At first her negativity was uppermost. She had not been out for weeks and had spent much of her days in bed and was so ill. But slowly she accepted and agreed to my promise. I left her in a very happy mood of expectation.

I phoned her every day and prayed with her over the phone: she was getting better!

The wedding came and she felt great, she went through the day forgetting she had ever felt ill, and for a week after she remained well, Then she remembered how ill she had been, started telling everyone how God had promised and delivered fitness to her just for the wedding and how wonderful He was to do it.

But then I suppose she must have reasoned she was a sick woman and that the healing was only for the wedding; I don't know, but soon I was called in again to apply her bottle of medicine, and I would end up again and again drained of my energy.

Pastoral visiting was often a joy, but all too often it was an exhausting experience, and I would feel completely flaked out sometimes for days after such an experience. I often recalled the pastoral lecture I had once at College when the professor said. "Some Ministers have to stand back from their people, they dare not get close to the people they try to help or they would either break down in tears or be exhausted. However there are Ministers who not only sit where the needy person sits, they will even get inside and live what the sufferer is going through. You must choose which road you will travel". He had told us. I was one who shared, and sat where they sat.

The answer to Mrs Greatly was, I felt, that she had a negative attitude to her condition, and even enjoyed looking back at what doctors had said on hospital visits and the suffering she had endured. She got a pleasure out of her being ill,, and the sympathy she received from countless visitors made her afraid of changing from sickness to happy health.

I felt that it was only right and fair when discussing Healing Miracles to put this other side of the coin. Having dealt with that rather sad side of ministry, one can only leave it in confidence that God is an all loving God and the great joy, peace and sheer blessing He gives far out weighs our failures.

When I consider the thousands of occasions when I have conducted people to God's throne of

Grace in worship, and have known, without doubt, that people have been uplifted, guided, inspired, and taught, just by being in His presence, this more than compensates for the few times I would reckon as failures.

Chapter 26

FAITH SOMETIMES GETS HELP ALONG THE WAY

The custom is generally held that all the churches in a district will have a common meeting point through the 'Council of Churches'. Usually this Council is presided over by a President, either a local Minister or a Layman, and elected for a short period, perhaps one year or two years. When I came to retire the area I came to were rather short of Ministers, due to several moving away to other churches, and as it was the turn of a Minister to be President, I was asked to take that office. Even though I had only just retired there.

Perhaps it was because I was not very well known that the churches were a little cautious, but it was the custom for the incoming President to introduce something new, a kind of "Theme For The Year".

At their annual service, during my address I introduced the theme of Christian Healing. I explained that this had been practised in the Old Testament days, and also very much by Jesus, who had passed this ministry on through His Apostles and into the early church. It was still used today, and was part of the command of Our Lord to "Heal the Sick."

I proposed that during my year of office as President we should hold four healing services, one every quarter, and that lay people should be invited to join clergy in the 'Laying on of Hands' to any persons who came forward during the service for that purpose.

Although all churches acknowledge a Healing Ministry, it seemed that few, if any had practised it. There were doubts as to whether we should rush into this, doubts about how it would be done, and whether anyone would come forward anyway. At the following business meeting it was proposed that we might try just one Healing Service to see how it would be received. So I speedily arranged to get it into the first quarter.

I was a little amused by the way that everyone stood back as if they were afraid of this new thing, and seemed to think of me as the expert. As it happened it was my church's turn to host the coming Healing Service, which everyone seemed pleased about, and I chose one of my own Deacons to be a layman for the act of Laying on of Hands. I had no problem about the clergy being ready to take part.

The service was announced in each of the churches but no other advertising was done.

When the evening came I asked those taking part to spend a little time with me in the vestry and I made sure that all were happy with what we were going to do, and we prayed together.

The church was well filled, and I found myself wondering what had brought them; was it curiosity? Because it was something new to them? Or were there many sick who wanted healing? During worship I was careful to explain in some detail about the church's Ministry of Healing, and Our Lord's desire to heal the sick. Of the things that can cause barriers to healing, and what we were about to do, asking that those who did not come forward should pray for those who did.

When the moment came for those who wished, to come forward to have hands laid upon them, slowly at first, and then in a fairly long queue, people came. I had left as much space as possible between those laying hands, so that they could pray over each who came without disturbing others. People came and knelt, as it is not easy to lay hands on those standing up, they were asked if they wished to say anything about their need, and a quiet prayer was offered and hands were laid on each head.

Some had come of behalf of someone else who was ill, some just asked for God's Blessing. Most mentioned something that was troubling them and this made it important to pray for what ever they wanted praying about.

Sometimes I knew without being told just what the trouble was, and I was able to add to the prayer for them as The Holy Spirit made things known. The atmosphere was one of quiet prayerfulness and worship all over the church. There seemed to be a feeling that God was near, The Holy Spirit was at work, or certainly with us.

Following the service there were two things that happened. The next meeting of The Council voted to have the three other Healing Services, and these were arranged and duly held, in other churches in the area. The other thing which I felt important, was a very real and warm appreciation for the first service, which I think, helped other churches to see the importance of a healing ministry. Although I heard of no great miracles taking place, I did hear of people who had been healed and Blessed and of prayers being answered.

If one thinks of 'Healing Miracles' as occasions when people throw away their crutches and walk; although this undoubtedly does happen, it is not what I have usually experienced. But if your concept of Miracles is of God's intervention in a life to improve it, perhaps to stop a person leaning on some crutch or on someone else. Starting walking on their own two feet with God; then Miracles are often happening. But they are not often heard about. We do like to keep quiet about such things.

We have now entered the twenty-first century, and certainly older people can look back and see the great changes in society and within the church. By 'church' I do not mean buildings or organisations of course, but the true meaning of 'church' –groups of people committed to Jesus Christ, their ways of worship, and their propagation of The Gospel.

When I was young, that is the mid 1920s and the 1930s, most people went to church on Sundays, and everybody sought to live by, or at least acknowledged, Christian standards. What was right and wrong were understood by all and taught in detail from childhood, all from the Bible itself. Sunday, for an example, was to be kept holy, it was a day of rest, and very few people would ever consider working on a Sunday. Not even working at home, which meant that even washing lines and tools had the day off! Even the domestic staff had light duties on Sunday mornings and the afternoon free to rest and attend church.

The local newsagent would open for an hour or so to get the Sunday Papers out; and one Chemist in turn would open for two hours for prescriptions and items of healing only, all other shops and businesses were closed. Children would have quiet games to play with, we would listen to the radio, read, make music around the piano, go for walks, visit people, do jigsaws, and of course discuss the church service and the people we met there. There was usually Family Worship too.

Now I believe we are living in what The Bible calls "The Last Days". It won't be long now before Jesus will return: When the dead In Christ shall rise, and Believers alive at that time will be changed, all being taken up to be forever with The Lord.

How exciting a Miracle that will be!

But God also says in His Word that these Last Days will be terrible times to live through. Compared with the past these are terrible times. It says;- People will be selfish, lovers of money, boastful, proud, abusive, disobedient to parents, ungrateful, unholy, loveless, slanderous, without self-control, lovers of pleasure, adulterous.

That difference is noticeable today, we have thrown away the Ten Commandments, and have started Sunday Trading, allowed the building of pagan temples, and have stopped the teaching of the Christian Faith to our children. How I wish we could go back to those happy days, which through the past we enjoyed so much.

Personally I still live in that Christian way of course, like many others, I would not think of going to a shop to buy something on Sunday, or get my petrol on The Lord's Day. Every Sunday of my whole life, with very few exceptions, has seen me enjoying worship in a church. Oh what joy and happiness it has been being so close to Jesus and, my Father God. For me Sunday has always been the best day of every week, all my life.

All the old ways have now changed of course. The majority of the population in Britain are not Christian, although there are millions who are. This means that the majority have no set standard to live by, "they do that which is right in their own eyes" as The Lord says. This is likely to be the pattern for the coming days, as children are no longer brought up with the knowledge of their Creator and His Laws, they don't know what is right and wrong, what sort of world will it be when they grow up?.

This makes me very sad when I see what people are missing, here and now, and of course will miss for eternity when their time on earth is judged, and they are condemned. God and His people would not want Heaven to be like earth today. But it also gives me an inward thrill to see

278

the signs of the nearness of the end. Ever since I saw the people of Israel (the Jews) going back into The Holy Land I began to wonder if this was the fulfilment of the Scriptures, and a sign that these are The Last Days.

Then when I lived through their Six Day War and saw Israel back in Jerusalem I knew that it was the beginning of the end. Since then the daily news has from time to time told of events that were spoken of by Christ or the prophets, as signs of the nearness of Christ's return. I am a long way from being anything of a religious fanatic; I just enjoy reading The Bible and seeing it speak of things that are happening now. I look to see what else will happen. I feel as excited about the return of Jesus whom I love as I might be if I were awaiting the arrival of a lover who had written to say they were coming to see me.

It very much reminds me of the day at the end of the war when my brother sent a letter to say he was on the way home. He had managed to get out of Singapore and into India. Now we expected him home after all that time. His letter could have been written months ago, or only days, He might be still in India or already in England, was he on a plane or ship? He might walk in through that front door any minute; it might be months before he did. We read his letter again and again for clues, we speculated and discussed, but we just had no idea when he would come. But he was coming and that filled us with joy and anticipation after all those war years of absence.

The coming of Christ has the same feeling about it. We discuss and reason, some even believe that they have worked out the date, but we won't know until it happens and we see Him coming in the clouds of heaven with all the angelic host. Oh what a day that will be! To be changed in the 'twinkling of an eye', and to be caught up to be with Him, 'Forever '.

There are always folk who will scoff at the possibilities of things yet to happen. It has happened much within the last hundred years; from the 'Man will never fly' scoffers to the 'Space belongs to Science Fiction' brigade. Neither I nor anyone else knows the future, that's for sure. But Scripture prophecy has been challenged through every generation, but it has never been wrong.

Christ's first coming (Or Christ-mas) was fulfilled in every smallest detail; I believe His return will be perfectly fulfilled in every detail too. (And my idea is that it will be soon.) What a Miracle!

In my last fulltime church, before I retired, for several Christmases running I introduced a special service which became extremely popular and packed the church from floor to gallery. It started one year by organizing the children to play the familiar scene of The First Christmas. Mary and Joseph arriving to Bethlehem – to the coming of the shepherds and wise men. Nothing special about that.

But in the following years the church erected a platform in front of the pulpit so that the children could be seen. I built a backdrop of a stable with animals, which covered the pulpit, and I got older children to take the parts of the Christmas characters.

After the children were settled in the tableau we added the idea of what people might give Christ for His Birthday.

Various people walked up from the congregation with the tools of their trade. One might say "I am a carpenter, My Lord was once a carpenter, I give to him my talent, my skill, and the tools of my trade." The tools, a plane, chisel, and saw, were laid before the manger.

Another –"I am a driving Instructor, it is as important to teach people how to travel the road of life with Jesus as it is the roads of Britain, I give Him my talent, and pray that we all may learn to travel life's road taught by Jesus. I lay before Him The Highway Code, and the Bible. Life's Highway Code."

"I am a nurse....." "I am a teacher...." "I work for the Council to serve the community...."

So people came to leave at the manger the tools to represent their trade, each clearly labelled, and their dedication written clearly.

Interspersed with the well loved carols The Minister's brief message was also given as an offering of his ministry and a clerical collar left. The climax of the service was the offertory, each person was invited to leave their pew and come to view The Manger Scene, to see what others were offering to Jesus; then to place their offering in the plates provided, and to offer a brief prayer, offering themselves and what Jesus would like from them as His Christmas present this year.

Year after year the church would be packed from floor to gallery, and the stewards would guide the people down one side of the church to the front, and up the other side back to their seats. The lights lowered but light enough for people to see the words of the Christmas hymns they sang while all this was going on.

I was privileged to stand to one side at the front while the crowds moved slowly past the 'Manger', and see all that others were offering in their lives.

I saw the moving lips as the prayers to Jesus were offered; saw the tears roll down the cheeks, the light in the eyes, and the joy on the faces. I saw the deep love that was exchanged by many with their Lord and Saviour; I know that what I saw was very acceptable in His sight. This was for most of that crowd real worship, a sacred offering. A MIRACLE. They would remember through the coming years.

Then to place their offering in the plates provided, and to offer a brief prayer, offering themselves and what Jesus would like from them as a Christmas present this year.

From time to time such inspiring acts of worship do bless and encourage a Minister and people, but one must never forget that the average or general act of worship will probably hold a miracle or two that will never be known about. Just occasionally one will visit someone's home on a normal pastoral call and during the conversation it will come out that a certain sermon that was preached either last Sunday or perhaps two years ago, was received with great effect. Perhaps it even made a turning point in that person's life.

The plain fact is that no one can know what influence we have on those around us. I am a firm believer that God uses those men and women who walk close to Him to speak or communicate in some way His message for the needs of others, And we are blissfully unaware of it!

We are all transmitters. The smile on our face, the words we speak, and the way we say things, The things we do, the things we believe. In fact everything that we are influences other people. God can use those who are walking with Him to do great things in the lives of others.

A person writes a story, others have their part in publishing it in book form, people read it, someone makes a film from the story, it becomes popular, and added music with the story gets everyone singing. It is translated into other languages because others want to experience what has become popular. Soon the whole world knows that story, and it can influence everyone.

There is no way that any of us can know just what God Almighty will do with us and our unique personality. Walk with The Lord and make sure your influence is good.

Chapter 27

FUTURE CHURCH?

I was aged fifty-five when I moved into what would be my last full-time church ministry.

I well recall that before I accepted the call I met with The Deacons and we did a tour of the buildings. When we came to the Church Building itself I was standing near the main entrance door when I was asked "What changes would you like to see here in the future?" I remember just what I said, "I would like to see an all glass partition right across this rear part of the church and large glass doors instead of the present wooden ones, so that people could see into the church from outside, and a carpeted area greet people as they come in.

"It would be nice to see the church with wall-to-wall carpet and chairs instead of the old pews, and a neatening up of the front part of the church.

Oh and a nice attractive notice board outside that looks modern, easy to change and read." I noticed the look on the faces of some of the Deacons and hastily added, "Don't worry, it probably won't happen in my time."

I could somehow see just how attractive the church building could look. If you go to Kingswood Congregational Church Bristol today, you will see exactly what I envisaged that day, although it did not all happen in my time. I believe that God is enabling churches to modernize today as never before. Some churches are making the change out of necessity, for the cost of heating such lofty buildings is a treasurer's nightmare. The need to provide refreshments or a cup of tea or coffee after the service is a great help in getting the people together after worship. So where possible it is a good thing to pull down the crumbling old buildings before they become unsafe or too expensive to maintain; let a new one arise.

All this may sound common sense to most people, but when one explores the cost of such schemes, courage wanes! Where can a small congregation get large sums of money for such plans? They can only just manage to keep going week by week and to maintain the status quo. This is where Miracles come in. If I have heard it once, I have heard it many times: - "It all seemed impossible but we started praying, and talking about it, we started prayer meetings and we worked and somehow our prayers were answered".... "We believed that God would, and He did".

The modernisation of many church buildings is accomplished these days more in the miracle bracket than in ways that man can see.

The History of the Christian Faith, whether through its Old Testament roots, or through the days of its Creator, Jesus, or through the two thousand years of its trial and growth, is a story of God working His purpose out in ways that man cannot understand or see quite how He does it. This is a world of Miracles, and it will continue at all levels, from the meek and humble Christian soul receiving the mighty Grace of God, to the world wide events in the everyday.

Miracles take place under God's Sovereign power and purpose, but I have often wondered as to how much human 'Faith' has to be present. Does a miracle depend on our Faith? Or is a hoped for miracle a means to strengthening our Faith for the receipt of it? The teachings of Our Lord would strongly indicate that Faith was an essential to life, and He was surprised and amazed that His disciples had so little Faith.

The Apostles learned the importance of Faith, and in their letters to the early church they also indicate that Faith is a vital part of a Christian's life. "Without Faith it is impossible to please Him". The words of the hymn writer often set me wondering when we sing "If our faith were but more simple, we would take Him at His word, and our lives would be all sunshine in the richness of His word". I have come to believe that a believing, trusting Faith is essential to a happy and successful life, but when the testing time comes I have to confess how difficult it often is to hold on to the kind of Faith needed for the situation.

My mind goes back to my Retirement as a typical illustration. I recall that there was some kind of family discussion as I came up to sixty years old. I had not been well for some time and the decision was taken then that I should retire on my sixty-fifth birthday. This was the first feeling of panic I experienced. Where were we going to live and what would we live on?

289

My situation was poor as far as money was concerned to say the least. I had come into the Ministry after four years of earning nothing. The pay, (or stipend) of a Congregational Minister was very poor indeed, and my expenses included my wife and four children to support. Added to this I had needed to furnish a home and run a car (for health reasons as well as the work) so we were never able to put any money away for a rainy day. Of course it did rain! That is there were home replacements and school uniforms etc constantly coming up. Each church in which I ministered supplied a house for the period of my stay with them (The Manse) and when I left my last ministry to retire I would have nowhere to live, the house belonged to the local church....Panic!

My lifetime as a Christian told me to trust The Lord, He would provide. So I had Faith. But here was the problem, I was only human, living in a human world and every so often I would think "Where am I going to live?"...... "Do I really think that God is going to suddenly give me a house to live in." Where would it be anyway? After all my years the temptation to periodically panic was still around, "Yes" I told people and my church "I am retiring on my sixty-fifth birthday". ("I hope" I would think!)

How would you feel if you were in my position? I did not own a house, and would have to leave the one I was in, on the date set. I had no savings, and no rich relations!

Someone told me that our Congregational Federation had a small housing scheme but it would seem that there was little hope of my being able to obtain accommodation through this channel. I wrote to enquire, but heard nothing.

I put out a few feelers through various friends but my faith was to be tested much further it seemed. The thought also came to me that maybe retirement at sixty-five was not what The Lord wanted for me, quite a few people said "Ministers never retire", if no housing miraculously came did I have to beg the church to let me carry on and say I did not want to retire after all?

Coupled with this I found it difficult to discover what pension might be forth coming, the state pension that I had paid into since starting work at fourteen did not seem to be nearly enough, and this was particularly so as I had no idea what my expenses would be. "Don't Panic!" I told myself in a panic filled voice.

Have you noticed that when God provides for all our needs He doesn't give advanced notice what He intends to do so. Like the films and fiction stories, rescue comes only just in the nick of time. It was to be so over these five years of waiting.

Even when it came it was to present problems. Only months away from the retirement date I had a letter to say that The Committee had met to discuss my application and my need of housing and that I could choose a house up to a certain value and The Congregational Trust would consider buying it for my wife and I to live in, on condition I was prepared to agree to the Trusts terms and conditions.

After the dance of joy and jubilant feelings and Praise to God, we asked ourselves Where! We have no roots. Audrey and I were born in South East London but we had no connections there now, and it had all changed since we left all those years ago. I should have hated to live in London, and there was no thought of doing so now. The areas where I had ministered in the past had also changed and moved on, we knew a few church people but there were no feelings of going back. I felt strongly that it would be unwise for me to live in the present churches area, any new Minister they had would be cramped by the past Minister being in the district. Also there were no houses that would suit our price range in Bristol.

We started to make a few enquiries about the price of housing in different parts of the country. We could find no place South of Birmingham, where we could afford to go on the figure that was offered us. We started to pray more earnestly for guidance from our Heavenly Father.

In all such situations there is always a feeling that WE have to decide, that WE have to find a way out of the difficulty. The fact was that God had got it all planned and He knew just when I was to retire and had already told me that. He knew where He wanted us to live and what He wanted us to do. He had it planned to the last tiny detail. If only I had exercised my Faith I would have had a much easier time. Looking back I see that this has always been His way, why do I have doubts?

God wanted me in a place that I had never even thought of, but how was He going to tell me where to go?

I was counselling a wedding couple at the time and happened to say just as a matter of passing interest "Where are you going to live, have you got it all settled?" "Oh yes, we have got a little house in South Wales". "South Wales!" I said "Why do you want to go to live there? Your families, friends, work and interests are all here in Bristol, and you will have to cross the bridge every day to get to work" They smiled "It's a lovely place really and any way it was the only area in which we could afford to buy a house, housing is cheaper there, there was nowhere else we could go".

It was as if God had spoken!

We phoned various Estate Agents in the area across the Seven River, the land of South Wales, We poured over maps, and soon we were looking through information of property all around the M4 Motorway from Newport downward into the heart of the area. Soon we had quite a list of properties that were within our given price range.

We set off with great excitement for a day of house hunting in a land we knew nothing about. Our first attempts at house viewing were disappointing, the first being in a back street of Newport, front door straight onto the street, the rooms dark and very small and a very small back yard with an outside privy.

We rather liked Newport itself with its modern shopping complex and enjoyable shops. We stopped at a restaurant for coffee and were given free donuts. Driving further down the Motorway we started viewing better property, some of which we felt we could live in, but they were not quite what we should go for.

We were to make several trips across The Bridge, the toll at that time being only 50p. One day we found ourselves viewing houses in Cross Keys near Risca, but each time we felt that God was saying "No" to every one. It was a misty day and it seemed to fit our mood as we looked to see if we had missed any properties before returning home. There was one, we had seen it several times in the write-ups but did not think it would be suitable as it stated a sitting room and a dining room, which sounded rather like some we had seen which were two very small rooms. However we decided that as we were near we would just look at it.

It turned out to be the last house but one in a delightful cul-de-sac. The whole road had come in for a recent Council Scheme of Renovation and it was quite smart. The owner was a woman and little girl; her husband was a Customs Officer and had been transferred, so she was left alone awaiting someone to buy the house so that she could move to be with her husband. The house was charming; the Sitting room/Lounge was combined with the Dining Room making one large room, down stairs Kitchen and Bathroom, Small garden with rear entrance. Upstairs bedrooms and toilet were just right and we both felt straight away that This Was IT.

So it turned out to be. We visited it again a few days later when the mist had gone, and to our amazement discovered that we were surrounded by beautiful mountains. We knew that this was where God wanted us to go; some of the family saw it and agreed. We submitted our application to The Committee and in due time it became our home for the next ten years. When I say ten years this was not what we considered at the time, we both thought that this would be our last home, that we would be living there until our final call of God. That was not to be. But that is another story.

The point I should have learned was to have Faith In God when a situation seemed impossible. "Is anything too hard for The Lord?" asks scripture. We frankly thought this might be, We could not believe that our God could supply us with a house! This was too big a thing. We had entertained thoughts of "supposing He doesn't!" How will we manage if He fails us.

"Is anything too hard for The Lord?" The real answer is "NO!" "Why is it that you have no Faith?" Jesus once asked. He asks it still!

On the calendar my birthday was now also My Retirement Date. Bit by bit I was making progress for my departure from the church, but along side, Audrey and I were starting to prepare our new home. Soon the legal work was over, and we were given the keys, we made trips to the new home, the car always loaded. The buying and fixing up of curtains. (Old ones never fit) making a fishpond so that my gold fish could come too, getting the dog used to the new smells of Wales, and as we were moving to a smaller house there was the buying of new items of furniture where the old pieces would not fit in. And of course Packing! That always seems a mammoth task.

My son gave me a day or so helping dismantle my model railway, it had taken four to five years to build and it was dismantled in about three days. I gave him my special large shed which had been the Model Railway home, for it would never fit into the new garden area, and he was keen to have it. We had moved several times during my lifetime but each time it gets harder not easier. This time my son and friends were going to rent a moving van and do the actual moving, and I was most indebted to them for their time and efforts. It was all part of this particular miracle.

Chapter 28
WHAT A SEND OFF!

It is never easy to leave a church and say goodbye to so many wonderful people and the last act of worship together with my friends was a precious experience. The evening before my retiring birthday we were given a 'send-off', which started with 'The Town Crier' and included every department of the church giving us their thankful greetings and a gift to remember them by. Towards the end of the evening The Church Secretary concluded his speech by inviting all those who had joined the church since my coming, to come and stand with him, and a sizable crowd came and stood beside him. Then those who had been healed during my ministry, those who had had some special blessing, those I had married, and as each was called I was amazed to see how many God had influenced through my ten years spent there. It was not a sad evening in the end but one of triumph and praise to God for ten wonderful years of His work among them.

Then came the move to South Wales with the army of helpers for which we were so thankful and the unpacking, with a daughter staying for a few days to help us. She returned home and suddenly one morning I awoke to realise that I did not have to prepare for next Sunday, or visit anyone, or attend any committees, and I spent the days just pottering and exploring the wonderful new area, discovering new shopping places, building a new large pond for the goldfish, and just relaxing. But my Heavenly Father had other things for me to do and I was soon to discover just why He had performed this Miracle of re-housing us in that particular place.

Audrey and I decided that we would spend our Sundays visiting the various churches around us. There was a Congregational Church in nearby Risca which was being pulled down but there was a notice, which told us that it was transferred to the local Presbyterian Church just up the road, so this was our first to visit.

The service was held in the hall because this church was also going to be demolished, and when we got talking after the worship was over we discovered that the Congregational Church had become United Reform and had joined with the Presbyterians to make a new church, once the old Congregational Church in Risca was rebuilt both congregations would worship there and the church building we were in would be demolished and sold.

Our coming to worship with them that Sunday was considered as a Miracle because the two church Ministers had just left and they were desperate for a Minister to help them out with the conduct of worship for the Sundays that they could not find preachers. I was booked up at once for a number of Sundays, and those good people there were to be our friends over the coming years. We felt at once as if we belonged to our new community and it was a joy to be hailed in the street by friendly people that we knew right from the start of our coming to this new land.

On the Sundays that I was not preaching at this church we explored other churches to see where God might lead us to put our membership. It was not long before we visited The Congregational

Church at Cross Keys, I discovered that they had not had a Minister for over forty years, and I was invited to conduct their Harvest Services. After I had done this there was great enthusiasm for me to come and help them as much as I was willing to.

It was then that I was requested to attend the Council of Churches Meeting. But I explained that I had no right to do so as I was a new comer to the district and not yet a member of any church in the area. I was still urged to attend. When I did so I learned that the district had just lost four Ministers and that it was the turn of a Minister to be President of The Council, would I please take the position. After prayer I saw God's hand in all this so I accepted.

My fears over moving to a strange area and a Land where I did not expect to understand the language were completely lost as I now, within a few months, was known and accepted by many of the local people, was preaching most Sundays and now was President of The Council of Churches. Yes, here was yet another Miracle!

As part of my Presidential work I arranged for a Christmas Party for all the churches, which was run by the local Anglican Church and brought local

Christians together on a social basis, which was good. When the subject of The Lenten Study Course came up there were sighs of unhappiness for these had not been received well in the past few years, So I wrote a new course and got various people to help run it. It turned out to be a great success and they wanted, and got, more in the following four years.

It was a time of change in the churches with a new church and new Ministers coming into the area. The local Methodist Church in Risca closed rather suddenly and I helped to influence the joining together of those now without a church, joining the new joint church. For the ten years that Audrey and I were to be in Cross Keys we were able to help the local cause along and gained many wonderful friends.

I was able to serve several of our Congregational Churches in the South Wales area and take a full part in the Congregational Area work where retired Ministers were welcomed. The local Cross Keys Church, Trinity Congregational, who had not known a Ministry for years, then approached me with a view to my becoming their Part Time Minister. In considering this I could see several problems. One of these was the fact that I was not a fit man and there was a danger that if I undertook a part-time work it could easily develop into a full-time Ministry where I worked as much as I had before retirement without the help of the large congregation and with very little money to do it on.

I finally said "yes" on the strict condition that I would not do visiting work, and that certain problems were removed so that there would be an opportunity for my work to succeed.

This was accepted and I was inducted as Part Time Minister and I served in this capacity for five years until I was in my seventies, during this time I gave a Bible Teaching Ministry and did all I could to promote the work of Trinity Congregational Church Cross Keys. Audrey and I remained in membership, Audrey being a Deacon, until we were to leave the district.

When I ceased to be their Minister they were able to call another part-time man and he had much to give the church that I could not give. During the following years I served the local churches and many of those in the South Wales Area. I was out preaching most Sundays.

One of the mistakes we made was over language. I have always believed that when you go and live in another part, you become part of that area. "When in Rome do as Rome does" as the quotation goes. Now we were living in another country we had to become Welsh. We started evening classes learning to speak the Welsh Language, not an easy task! Here we ran up against a real problem, we could find no one who spoke Welsh. After a while we decided to give the idea up as everyone around us spoke English, albeit with a Welsh Accent!

The second thing I learned was a little bit of Welsh History and this has made me ashamed to be English. As an Englishman I never knew what we had done to the Welsh. We walked into their country, slaughtered their Royal Family and Princes, and enslaved their people. We have kept them in poverty ever since. Little wonder that The Wonderful Welsh People often have no love or trust in the English. At last the coalmines are gone and much of the squalor, South Wales is now blossoming into a beautiful country and it has lovely people. I feel angry that the English have little understanding or care for the Welsh, the

Scots, or the Irish; we have treated them, and still treat them very badly. I am not proud to be English any longer. Especially as we have now just about lost Britain to the domination of Europe.

I dismount this hobbyhorse to continue our great theme of Miracles, and one that deserves mention shows that our wonderful Lord has concern for even the smaller things of life.

Chapter 29
THERE ARE SMALL MIRACLES TOO

As I have mentioned I have enjoyed the hobby of Railway Modelling since the nineteen-sixties and when we moved into the house in Wales there seemed no place where I could build a layout .On a discussion with my son it seemed that the only place at all was in the loft which would certainly house a good size one, but it was too cold in the winter and far too hot in the summer.

The Lord knew all about this but I did not ask for guidance as there did not seem to be any answer to the problem, so why ask The Lord to do what you consider impossible! How often we take this attitude!

I needed something stored in the attic one day and went in search. To my alarm I found a small pool of water up there. Now the house had been re-roofed only three years before and the surveyors had given it all a detailed inspection, how could it leak? I notified The Trust who sent the surveyor to look into it. He was mystified and assured me that there was no leak, then he found the cause, it was condensation. The insulation on the floor was too poor; heat is getting through from the house and hitting the cold roof, the cure? "you must have all new insulation."

I don't know what made me ask him but I asked "Does it matter whether the insulation is on the floor or the roof of the loft?" "No" he told me. After further discussion with my son I phoned the Trust to tell them the news and offered we would re-insulate the area if they would pay for the material, this was agreed upon and with the help of some of the family we put the insulation material up onto the roofing felt above, enclosing it with hardboard sheets (which we paid for) The result was a large area of loft space cool in the summer and warm in the winter in which I built the largest and best Model Railway layout I had ever had. Is anything too hard for The Lord?

Of course it took several years to build in my spare time but when finished I was able to photograph it and use the material to have articles published in the Model Railway Press. Known as "The Saint Francis Island Railway" it became quite famous. Running ten full passenger trains and twelve goods trains to timetable and to sound.

Although this was a delight to me Our Father always likes to add something very special. I had foolishly been wondering if it might be possible to get onto television with The Gospel, The Christian programmes on Television were so poor, I felt they could be done better (Big Head!) Suddenly I had a phone call from a producer at the B.B.C. who wanted to know if I could show my Model Railway on a programme he was producing. The programme was a rather silly thing I later thought, about grown up people attached to things that children use, and he had got my name from the editor of the railway magazine where I had published articles.

Following his visit he realised that I could tell a good story as well as show the best railway model he had seen (perhaps he had not seen many) so a day for filming was arranged.

A fleet of cars arrived at 9am in the morning and left around 10pm that evening with several cans full of film. They were delighted that I turned out to be a 'One Take' man and not an inch of film was lost on retakes. I sat through interviews and told two or three stories. Then we squashed into my loft space. Producer, cameraman, camera, several sets of lights and me. I ran trains, phoned the signal box up the line and held a conversation, (via my tape recorder) talked about the layout, was shot going up the loft ladder, coming down the loft ladder, and even Audrey was filmed seemingly bored downstairs: and finally they removed the mass of cables and equipment and left.

On Christmas Eve at peak viewing time 9pm on B.B.C.2 I watched the programme. Most of their days work had ended on the cutting room floor, but I did tell one story and did have about twenty minutes on screen, so my fame came, it burnt itself out, and is forgotten. But for me there was that wonderful voice of God afterward "Now you know that I could put you on television if I wanted to, but this is not my will for you." In its way it was a miracle to me, but I have learned that God can do all these things if He wants to, and I have broadcast one service, run a short series of radio programmes and achieved most of the so called big things, but they come and they go, and they are forgotten. There is nothing either great or small that God cannot arrange for a person to do if He wants it that way, but as the Bible says in Ecclesiastes "Vanity, vanity, all is vanity". I am glad I am a little unknown nothing, that will soon be forgotten!

When I was graciously granted the occupation of the house in Wales Audrey and I considered that this was where the end of the road would be for us. Audrey took great delight in walking the mountains and valleys and it seemed that we had all that anyone could ask of life, we were very happy there. We would grow old and be carried out in a box.

I told my neighbour "We are here for the rest of our days", and we really thought that was so, I did not know it could be any other way. But God had other ideas that we knew nothing about.

It was during a family get-together, and we were enjoying general conversation that suddenly it was said that it was a great pity that we lived here in Wales. The cost in money and time made it more and more difficult for the family to visit us. It was true that since the Seven Bridge had been taken over by a European company the cost had gone up and up, ten fold what it had been. And the cost of petrol was constantly rising. But apart from this it was over an hour each way for our son and his family to come to us and an hour and a half each way for one daughter and nearly four hours each way for the one in London.

"What is going to happen when you both get older" we were asked "How can we care for you? You need to live close to one of us". My attitude was that it was not possible to do anything about it, we had been blessed to have a house to live in, and when we had made the decision of Wales it had been the only place we could have considered. We would just have to trust that nothing untoward would happen. God would look after us.

It was just after this that I had to phone the secretary who was in charge of the housing trust. The matter I phoned about being concluded I remarked that he must be having an easy time at present and his reply was to show me a solution to the very problem that the family had raised.

"I am extremely busy" he replied. "I have three men moving, one into a property we have just bought for him and the other two moving from their existing trust property to another".

I told him "I did not know it was possible to change a house once we had been given one". "Well" he said "We don't make a practice of it, but where there are very good reasons we will, One of our men had lost his wife and is going into a small flat we are buying for him, the other is moving to be near his family".

I wrote to the trust explaining that we would like to move nearer one of our children so that they could look after us in time of need, and it was agreed that we should look for such a possibility. We were given a slightly better price for them to buy such a house which also made it possible. But where would we go?

With a daughter and family in Canada, a son in Bristol, a daughter in Taunton Somerset and the other daughter in London the choice fell between Bristol and Taunton. We would hate to live in London. We prayed for the guidance needed and started looking in Bristol and Taunton.

After a great deal of house searching in Bristol God slammed the door firmly for this direction. We discovered what the Bristol Rates were, and knew at once that our monthly income could not run to that, and the houses we had seen were not at all what we were looking for. Later my son Peter was to move to Frampton Cotterell with his family, so it proved to be the right choice for us to look to Taunton. God knows what He is doing!

Once again we started to obtain details of houses, this time in the Taunton area. We visited the area several times to view property always looking for the place that God was saying "Yes" to. Twice we found a place we thought Might Do, but on both occasions we did not feel that these were what God was saying "This is it". And then it came. There was one house that we had seen advertised but did not go for straight away. The floors were of wood and we had always been used to carpeted floors. However we decided to look at it, and although it was smaller, as was most of the homes we had seen, it was The One; and we have kept the polished wooden floors!

There was some work to do on the property; a down-stairs toilet was built, a banister fitted on the stairway, and things like that. From the upstairs bed room we have a lovely view of farm land and distant scenes, the nearest field usually filled with cows. The garden is far better than we have had before, and in order to cut out mowing grass we had the front lawn covered with lining and filled with shingle; and we gave our mower away.

My daughter, who is nursing at the local hospital, is only ten minutes drive away, and we see as much of her and the family as we both wish. It is God's answer. We are all set up for the future, another Miracle as far as we are concerned.

So here we are. Yes we do have things we have to suffer, and my ill health restricts my activities. Audrey has her share too, but we are glad to be so richly Blessed.

We are members in the local Congregational Church, where once I Ministered, Audrey has been called as a Deacon and is busy in the churches work. Everyone shows love to us, and we help in a church group mainly for senior citizens. I lead Bible Studies and the testimony of those who have attended is that "I make the Scriptures live, and they feel as if they had been present as the Bible events unfurl". Praise indeed!

I contribute two or three articles every month to the Church Magazine. We work well with the Minister here and I try to be as helpful as I can without usurping his authority. Yes, Miracles still happen. Healings still take place, But The Father in Heaven and I just smile over them and say nothing now. I don't ask Him for much, He already supplies more than all we need, but I know that when I do ask Him I always seem to receive, and His delivery service is second to none. Our Life is a Miracle!

And here is the last true story. As I was checking this manuscript my computer developed a fault and nothing that Microsoft or anyone could do could bring it back to life. I argued with myself that it was not the thing to do, to pray about a computer.

But I did. I sat quietly in God's Almighty presence and asked Him to heal whatever was wrong and restore it. I opened my hands and held them over the laptop. Switched it on and it came on, booted up and has been working on and off all day perfectly. I knew He could, I believed He would, and He has done what I asked.

So I wrote this final piece. I accept that there is nothing that my God cannot do. May you also welcome Him fully and completely into your daily living and find an ever closer relationship with your Father and Saviour as His Spirit lives within you.

"Faith is... being sure of what we hope for, quite certain of what we do not see."
This is what all God's people are commended for. (Hebrews Ch11.)

Gerald Gossage

Printed in the United Kingdom
by Lightning Source UK Ltd.
117948UK00001B/283-291